21 LESSONS LEARNED
IN SALES MANAGEMENT

21 LESSONS LEARNED IN SALES MANAGEMENT

TED KULAWIAK

Palmetto Publishing Group
Charleston, SC

First Edition

Printed in the United States

ISBN-13: 978-1-64111-827-9
ISBN-10: 1-64111-827-X

THIS BOOK IS DEDICATED TO:

Robin, Carin, Justin, Bastian, Grammie, Gramps, Mom, Dad, Chris, Michelle, Pumpkin, Corey, and Missy. I could not ask for a better family.

Debbie Dingerson Cole, because I promised her in high school that I would dedicate my book to her. I haven't spoken to her in thirty-plus years, but a promise is a promise.

Richard "Dick" Stern, my first sales manager, a true gentleman and professional, who provided a positive influence on my life when I was just starting out in sales.

Greg Linnerooth, who opened my eyes to the people side of a business by allowing me the freedom to live and learn, fail and succeed, laugh, and laugh some more while setting the example with his great sense of humor and caring.

John Holbrook, Dave Pauldine, and Steve Riehs, owners of their respective themes, *The Power of One, Don't Settle for Mediocrity*, and *Let the Data Direct the Decision-Making*.

Adrian Marrullier, without question the most intelligent and creative marketer I've worked with during my career.

Last but not least, my brother **Ken Kulawiak**, who taught me how to ice skate, shoot a hockey puck, throw a baseball, swing a golf club, cast a fishing line, build models, and play poker, cribbage, and board games, and who, in general, is the epitome of what a big brother should be.

CONTENTS

FOREWORD

I always knew I would write a book, but I never really knew what that book would be about. After forty-plus years in the sales environment, working for several different companies in a few different industries, I finally figured it out. Those of you who are not salespeople may find humor in that statement, depending on your view of salespeople and the sales profession. I do not claim to be an expert in the sales field, but I will say that I am proud of my profession and my ability to earn a nice living in an ethical manner, assisting people in meeting their needs. My experience as a senior faculty member teaching Sales Management at DeVry University's Keller Graduate School of Management, significantly complements my sales management foundation and contributes to the anecdotes and principles in the book.

21 Lessons Learned in Sales Management is about my experiences in sales and sales management, offers some foundation on what I consider to be the key principles of remarkable sales management, provides a few tidbits that you may use in your own day-to-day business endeavors, and hopefully will also provide humor for you.

I couldn't help myself, however, and had to add my opinion about some other non-sales-related subject matters.

I titled the book as such simply because everything you read here is based on my opinion and interpretation of sales lessons learned. I've lived by the premise that I will not offer advice to people; although many seek as much, I always counter with the fact that I don't offer advice, only opinion. Advice puts too much burden on the provider and can cause too much grief for the recipient. Opinion is just that…it's what I think and offer. Offering opinion instead of advice allows the recipient to make their own decision regarding matters, and isn't that the way it should be?

Anyway, please note that while I have a journalism degree, I never really practiced the profession for which I studied in college. As a matter of fact, I hardly studied in college at all, and maybe that's why it took me so long to get going on the book. The fact is I always enjoyed writing and want you to know that my writing style, if you haven't guessed already, is plain and simple. I hope you find this book to be an easy read, yet one that provokes a thought or two. While there is quite a bit about sales management in this book, I hope you enjoy the anecdotes and breaks from the main subject matter. Most of all, I hope you enjoy the opportunity to form your own opinion on whether you agree with me or don't agree about my opinions in the book. That's the whole concept, because that's what this book is about: opinion on sales management.

Enjoy.

LESSON 1: INSPECT WHAT YOU EXPECT

*You cannot build a reputation on the
things you are going to do.*

My first real job out of college way back in 1977 was selling dis-play advertising for the *Suburban Life Citizen* newspaper, part of Life Printing and Publishing, a chain of local newspapers in the western Chicago, Illinois, suburbs and at that time a very highly credible and reputable firm. Life Printing and Publishing and its successors has long since been absorbed by mass media or-ganizations during the media consolidation period and downfall of newspapers in general, having been replaced by much more timely social media options. We want our news instantly, as it happens, and the advances in technology certainly provide that to us currently. Yet, for some people, there was—and perhaps still is—a certain legitimacy to having the news in hard print. For my generation, reading the daily newspaper was the norm. It was a way of life. Working for a newspaper at that time was a worthwhile endeavor, which taught me quite a bit about selling to different types of people and personalities, and their variety of businesses.

With a journalism degree from Northern Illinois University and fully ready to put it to use, I had applied via letter and résumé to numerous advertising agencies, newspapers, and magazines in the Chicago area. No takers. I had a few, very few, interviews but just couldn't get anyone to hire a "rookie" right out of college with no experience. I applied for writing jobs, copy jobs, circulation jobs—anything and everything that would help me get my foot in the door and start on a career in the newspaper business. Nothing. Then I got some much-needed help. It turned out that my mother attended church with a friend of one of the owners of the company. My mom's friend (I only knew her as Mrs. Ondrus) owned a business in Berwyn, Illinois, and was an advertiser in the Life newspapers. She did my mom a favor and arranged for me (via part owner Jack Kubik) to meet with the *Suburban Life* general manager, Richard "Dick" Stern, at his office in LaGrange Park for an interview. I had no specific job in mind, just the opportunity to talk to a person whom I would later come to respect as my first manager, leader, mentor, coach, and role model.

When I walked into Mr. Stern's office, it was easily recognizable as one of a "newspaperman." He wore thick black-framed glasses, white shirt, and a tie buttoned to the collar. He had a closely trimmed head of gray hair and no facial hair. His office smelled of cigarette smoke. His habit of smoking two-plus packs per day was ingrained. Newspapers were piled two feet high on the credenza behind his Steelcase desk, the left side of which butted up against the cinder-block side wall of the office. The side opposite of the cinder-block wall was glass from ceiling to midwall. The room itself was no larger than twelve feet by twelve feet. There was one wooden chair across from Mr. Stern's desk set at a ninety-degree angle, so if you sat proportionately in it the way it was placed with your back to the side wall, Mr. Stern would be sitting at your three o'clock. There were three other chairs placed against the far wall directly opposite his desk. It looked like a lineup waiting area for the dentist. No conference table for discussion. No comfy sofa, no lounge chairs, no refrigerator, no artwork. Bare walls, industrial carpet. The only "decoration" was the trash can to the side of the desk. This was functional, Spartan decor, to say the least. *Yet this "office," as I would later learn, was perfect for the man who occupied it daily and not only reflected his priorities but also served as a message to his sales staff. Mr. Stern was all business.*

As it turns out, there was an opening for a display advertising sales trainee, and to this day, I firmly believe the only reason I got the job was because of my answer to one of Mr. Stern's questions. After a series of the usual basic interview questions, he asked me what I wanted to do with my journalism degree. My answer got me the job. I told him I wanted to get into the business aspect of the newspaper. I wanted to learn the business and was not really interested in writing. That was enough to sell him. I believe he was just waiting for someone to come into his office other than the stream of idealistic next great newspaper editors whom he had been interviewing over the past month. *He wanted someone to learn to sell display ads. I just wanted a job. We both got what we wanted.*

Monday through Friday and every other Saturday morning, the sales staff reported into the office by 8:30 a.m. sharp. Monday was critical because that's when the sales staff, all six of us, including our display ad layout artist, would crowd into Mr. Stern's office for our weekly meeting. Dick Stern rule number one: be on time. If you were late, you did not enter Mr. Stern's office. You waited until the meeting was over and then walked into his office with your tail between your legs and apologized for your tardiness. You would have to catch up on what occurred in the meeting from the other salespeople. The best thing about learning promptness for a twenty-one-year-old right out of college was that it stuck with me throughout my career. I built part of my reputation by being on time, all the time and can count on one hand when I did not live up to that expectation. Second best was the way Mr. Stern handled every situation where someone for whatever reason came in late and missed the sales meeting. He understood. He accepted the apology and moved on. He didn't have time to make a big deal out of it. It's not that he didn't care. He already delivered the message by barring you from the meeting. He cared about what went on from that point. Even though you would be let off the hook, you knew it wasn't right to disrespect his request. He deserved better, so it was very seldom that one of the sales team missed a Monday meeting.

Once the meeting ended, if it was Monday, and then at least by 9:00 a.m. every other day, the sales staff was expected to either be on the phone calling customers, making appointments, or making calls on customers out in their territory. While there was no typical day, it was acceptable to be back in the office between 4:00 and 5:00 p.m. to prepare for the next day or do any follow-up work with accounts that needed to be accomplished. Dick Stern expected us to get out of the office, do our respective jobs, sell advertising space, and promote the newspaper with local business owners, and we did so with a level of trust and flexibility that we appreciated immensely. We had personal freedom while maintaining a level of dignity and importance. In other words, he treated us as professionals, and it was certainly easy to return that respect to a man who embodied hard work, dedication, fairness, and leadership.

We had daily freedom. We could report in for morning coffee, and then go about our day at our speed and come back later in the day for a regular recap. No one looking over our respective shoulders. No one micromanaging us. No one monitoring our every move. Not a bad gig. Just do your job and show up when expected. Certainly, this is a solid management style and at least provides a potential foundation for happy employees—a creed by which organizations should build upon that will hold true to this day.

Except there was just one thing of which I was unaware. While I respected Mr. Stern and his management style, I did not realize the extent of his reach. After all, he was in the office nearly all the time; he rarely went out on a sales call with me or the other sales reps. I can remember being with him to meet with the new marketing director at LaGrange State Bank, and a few brief meetings with other business owners in my territory. That was it. That was the extent of him working with me in the field. I spent more time learning how to sell from the other salespeople—or at least that's what I thought for some time. Then it hit me. Remember, I was only twenty-one and raw to the bone as far as experience and ability to read people. Dick Stern was so ingrained in the community that all he had to do to check up on any one of us was to make a phone call to one of his numerous contacts for the lowdown on how we were doing our jobs. He had people in places where we didn't even know the places existed. He practiced the art of "Inspect What You Expect" to a level of perfection and detail to make any sales manager envious. And did I learn a lesson.

While the majority of business owners in my territory were professional and courteous to a young trainee barging in on their business day to ask whether they were going to run an ad that week (mind you, there was not much selling skill there; it was just order taking to start), there were a few curmudgeons who wouldn't give me the time of day. They rarely advertised in our paper, spent quite a bit of ad dollars with the competition, and were just plain rude. I remember standing in front of one of these business owners for what seemed like an hour asking questions with no response, offering examples of advertising options with no response, showing artwork and editorials and news that was pertinent to their business with no response, and finally walking out dumbfounded that anyone who owned a business could be so rude and disengaged with a person just trying to do his job. Those "customers" were not on my regular call list. I avoided them like the plague after several attempts. I was tired of being treated rudely and tired of not selling anything to these select accounts. I gave up.

And Mr. Stern knew it. He knew I stopped calling on these accounts because he himself had talked to these owners. He called them when they ran ads in our competitors' publications, and while they weren't going to buy from us now, he paved a little bit of road for possible advertising in the future. They talked to him out of respect for him and his reputation. They knew him. They had no clue who I was. He wanted to know if I had been in to see them recently, called on them for the regularly scheduled local business promotions like Sidewalk Sale, Moonlight Madness, Back to School—any and all special promotions. And they told him. He didn't go behind my back. On the contrary, he was way ahead of me. He was always in front of the selling situation by practicing the age-old rule of Inspect What You Expect. He expected me to call on everyone and anyone in my territory who could possibly buy advertising space. Regardless of whether they bought something at that time, he expected me to work my territory to the fullest by calling on friends and nonfriends alike. He didn't even have to get out of the office to find out if I was doing the basic newspaper display advertising selling job of canvassing every business.

Dick Stern was the world's greatest sales secret shopper of all time. If he asked you straight up if you called on Mr. Floyd's Men's Clothing store for the upcoming promotion, you knew he had you. You couldn't say yes because he knew you would be telling a fib. If you said no, at least you were being honest, but then you'd better prepare yourself for a discussion about understanding the challenge of sales…take no and keep on trying. Don't give up. Don't give in. Diplomatically continue to pursue because this was the expectation. The worst that could happen was to hear "no," and you had to get used to that in sales. You had to grow thick skin and chalk that up as another opportunity to get one step closer to the account that would say yes.

A sales manager must have thick skin as well and come to the realization that even the best of salespeople will waver from the rigidity of expectations. That's one of the reasons why people get into sales; they like the freedom and flexibility. Salespeople like to be their own bosses. So it should come as no surprise that they will use that independence as a way of doing their job. And the sales manager needs to understand, perhaps even *encourage*, in some instances, the freedom for the salespeople to "do their thing" without getting in the way. However, that should not downplay the importance of the sales manager being engaged, involved, and active in the selling process by being in communication with customers and "knowing" what's going on with his or her team during conducting business. The need to know is part of being on top of the situation.

The example I provided to you is one from quite a long time ago but still holds true as foundation and lesson learned. Regardless of whether you are an outside sales manager with a large territory, or an inside sales manager operating in a call center, the objective is to pay attention to who, what, where, when, why, and how your salespeople are engaged with your customer base. This is not micromanagement. This is the concept of being aware of what's occurring under your watch!

During my career in sales management, I had the opportunity to manage and lead both outside territory and inside call center sales teams. In outside sales, I managed a seven-state territory with nine representatives who were true "road warriors," being on the road making sales calls in their assigned territory overnight three to four days a week and home for the remainder of time. It would have been very easy for me to sit back in my comfortable office every day and "manage" those hard-working representatives. And if I did that, I would have been viewed as a manager who didn't care enough to get out of the office and make sales calls with the team. Getting out of the office and working with territory representatives allows the sales manager the opportunity to meet with customers, spend time training and coaching the representatives, build relationships with both representatives and customers, and learn what's going on in the territory. It is an Inspect What You Expect moment.

Same thing in a call center, whether it is inbound, outbound, or web-based chat, I had the opportunity to lead and manage all types of these scenarios. At one time, I was accountable for six call centers in three different states with nearly one thousand people in my responsibility. That adds up to tens of thousands customer contact calls every week. If I didn't have a great group of sales managers with whom to work, there is no way I could have truly known what went on in each of my call centers. While I would listen to calls and spend time with my salespeople as often as I could, I had to rely on a highly skilled and dedicated team of sales managers who engaged in Inspect What You Expect daily. They listened to calls, engaged with customers, provided feedback, documented discussions, and, all in all, did what effective managers do: They paid attention to the team, the customers, and the business.

It sounds simple to Inspect What You Expect; it's pretty much a cliché statement and a given in management, but it's a difficult "must do." With all the distractions and pressures on the manager to deliver results, there can be a tendency to work from behind the desk and hope for the best. You may be asking yourself right now, "Who really does that?" but then also ask yourself "When was the last time I worked with and scheduled time on the calendar to make sales calls with my salespeople?" Working with your salespeople or call center representatives should be a given. It should be regularly scheduled and ingrained in your calendar. It should take precedence over administrative meetings.

You have an obligation as a sales manager to spend time observing, training, coaching and developing your sales team. You have an obligation to your company to know your customers, to spend time with them understanding their point of view, their concerns, their challenges. And you have an obligation to yourself to be the most involved, engaged, dedicated and knowing manager-leader that you can be. Take the time to Inspect What You Expect, and it will pay dividends throughout your managerial career.

Dick Stern taught me early on in my life to pay attention to the sales team and be involved with the customer base to provide a solid approach to managerial success. He did both and did them with professionalism, courtesy, intelligence and a high level of people skills. He was a pleasure to work with, learn from, and be loyal to, and he provided support when needed. He epitomized a role model, manager, leader, and confidant.

I really believe the thing he loved most, along with his family and fishing, was the career he chose as a newspaper general manager, which gave him an opportunity to enjoy work, be great at what he did, and coach others to be their best.

Working from that Spartan office, cigarette in one hand, phone in the other, Dick Stern loved what he did with a level of enthusiasm most sales managers could only imagine. He was the perfect first manager for me. He was what I emulated to be throughout my career (minus the cigarettes): well liked, but more importantly, admired for his ability to lead and build loyalty.

I miss his jokes, his stories—especially his fishing stories—his friendship, and his mentorship. I can still hear him calling out "Theo!" when he wanted me to come into his office. I miss how he taught me the basics of building the newspaper and doing a layout of where the display ads would be and partnering with the editorial team to give them the required space for their news articles. I miss that time in my life but relish the thought I had a great opportunity to start my career with a man who cared about me as a person as much as he wanted me to be successful. Dick Stern was a great person.

He had a massive heart attack during the final year that I worked at the newspaper, made a recovery, and came back to work several months before I left to move on to my career at 3M. I gave him a Muskie fishing rod on my final day at the newspaper as my way of saying thanks for giving me a start in business and for teaching me the valuable lesson of Inspect What You Expect.

Dick Stern died a few years later at the young age of fifty-four.

LESSON 2: CREATE A PROGRAM MANTRA

The man who rows the boat seldom has time to rock it.

Philip John Fleck, P. J. for short, is the head football coach at the University of Minnesota. I don't know P. J. Fleck. Never met the man. But I know of him and of his accomplishments. I also know that we share at least two things in common. First, we both earned our undergraduate degrees from Northern Illinois University. (Go Huskies!) Second, we both understand the importance of creating and implementing a program mantra.

Coach Fleck starred on the NIU football team as a too-small-to-be-any-good five-feet-ten wide receiver who earned second team Academic All-American during his senior year. He still holds the school record for punt returns (87), is second in school history in punt return yards (716), ranks third in career catches (179), and is fourth in receiving yards (2,162). He was twice voted team captain by his teammates. While coach Fleck had a brief stint with the NFL's San Francisco 49ers, injuries limited his ability to play professionally, thereby directing his attention to a coaching career.

He began his coaching career in 2006 at Ohio State as an assistant working with head coach Jim Tressel and then returned to NIU in 2007 under head coach Joe Novak and then his successor, Jerry Kill. Other stops included a stint in 2010 at Rutgers University with head coach Greg Schiano, back to NIU in 2012 with head coach Dave Doeren, and then on to the NFL's Tampa Bay Buccaneers, and in the same year, reunited with Greg Schiano.

The reason I included a brief summary of Coach Fleck's career path through 2012 is to point out the names of the head coaches with whom he worked. Everyone needs mentors, teachers, leaders from whom they can learn and develop and whom they can emulate. Coach Fleck's path provided him with the opportunity to work with and learn from some excellent coaches and mentors. (More on the importance of having a great mentor in a later lesson.) I'll bet if we were to ask Coach Fleck about his assistant coaching career, he would say that he was fortunate to work with and learn from such a diverse and talented group of individuals. I'll also bet that as a head coach, Fleck is aware of his opportunity to provide leadership, guidance, and mentorship to players, assistant coaches, and basically anyone associated with the University of Minnesota football program much as he did at his prior head coaching position at Western Michigan University.

It wasn't easy in the beginning for coach Fleck at WMU in 2013. He took over a losing program and promptly delivered a 1–11 record his first season. Yep, one win, eleven losses. That season only provided motivation for improved performance in the coming years. Coach Fleck knew what needed to be done to get the WMU program to a respectable level, and he placed emphasis on recruiting great players to WMU. Always Be Recruiting: Coach Fleck lived that lesson and enhanced it to its fullest by recruiting top talent that ranked his next three recruitment classes as among some of the best classes in the nation for midmajor football programs. His efforts paid off...big-time. WMU had four consecutive years of having the highest ranked recruitment class in the Mid-American Conference. When Coach Fleck left WMU after the 2016 season to accept the head coaching position at the University of Minnesota, the WMU team he developed finished their regular season 12–0. Yep, twelve wins, zero losses, including a 45–30 win over our alma mater, which marked the first time since 2008 that WMU beat NIU. WMU won the MAC Championship game, were ranked number 12 in the Associated Press College Football Poll, participated in the 2017 Cotton Bowl Classic versus then-ranked number 8 Wisconsin (a close game lost 24–16), and Fleck was named the MAC Coach of the Year. Pretty darned good change of direction from being 1–11 and not even on the college football competitive map to 12–1 and Coach of the Year with national exposure.

Somewhere along the way, during his time at WMU, Coach Fleck introduced the program mantra of "rowing the boat." Now I am not sure if he picked that premise up from one of his mentors, or he tweaked something from another program or if he thought of the "rowing the boat" mantra himself. All I know is that Head

Coach P. J. Fleck owns the terminology. In more ways than one. Turns out WMU licensed the phrase during coach Fleck's time there. So, enter the lawyers, the negotiations, and the discussions. WMU settled to use "Row the Boat" associated with the 2016 MAC championship team, and Coach Fleck settled to use the mantra at UM in exchange for an annual scholarship payment to WMU. Both sides won. More importantly, Coach Fleck's program mantra moved forward as a rallying cry for the UM program.

Rowing the Boat, for all intents and purposes, basically means never give up. It represents the concept of all team members pulling together...or, literally, rowing together...for a single cause. The focus is unified, the results are dependent upon each other, the direction is visible, the vision is clear. This simple yet profound mantra is at the core of Coach Fleck's charismatic approach to football coaching. He leads via a rallying cry that unifies all involved to put forth their best effort. Never give up. Keep pushing forward. All on the same page, all in unison, all having each other's backs. All emotion, mental, physical, spiritual whatever...all as a team. I love it!

If you need a little bit further clarification, I suggest you take a few minutes and watch the Olympic Men's or Women's Eight Rowing Final from 2018 on You Tube. There, you will see remarkable precision and teamwork and certainly will get your competitive juices flowing.

Once again, you're probably wondering why I am off on a tangent about crew and how this relates to sales management.

Besides being a great football coach, the enthusiastic and ever-positive P. J. Fleck delivered a message to his teams that is easily transferable to the daily sales management effort. You need a vision message on which to build. You need a mantra to rally the troops. You need a premise, a foundation, a Standard Operating Procedure on which to focus your team's attention. You need a consistent, unifying message to keep everyone in the sales department focused on performing to their utmost level while ensuring all are diligently persisting profitable revenue growth. You need a message that invigorates and motivates the team to perform to win. You need this message to be clear, visible, repeated daily, lived religiously, and bandied about with fun and adoration at the same time. You need a SOP to *win*!

During my time with DeVry, I created the direction of student-focused enrollment as the admissions team standard operating procedure. In support of the SOP, I used the letters *S*, *O*, and *P* to provide foundation to that direction. *S* stood for Sense of Pride. *O* stood for Ownership of Results. *P* stood for Professionalism.

This message was prominently displayed throughout our organization and specifically in the admissions offices that I led. Every management meeting, every new hire training, every end-of-class session included this premise. It was ingrained in our attitude, our performance, our way of being, and most importantly in our respect for each other and for our students.

Student-focused enrollment in a nutshell:

Sense of Pride: Be proud of your profession. Be the best at what you do; always put forth your best effort. When you start your day, start it with enthusiasm and a positive forefront that sets the tone and guides you for the rest of the day. When you leave work for the day, take pride in knowing you put forth your best effort and feel good about yourself. Always remember that you are helping others achieve their goals and fulfill their dreams, and that is a great foundation on which to take pride.

Ownership: Be accountable to yourself and your coworkers for your results. You, and only you, are responsible for your actions, your effort, your determination, your performance. No excuses. No blame sharing. No finger pointing. Be thankful and celebrate when you achieve your goals. Should you fall short of your goal, learn from the experience, and know that you will continue to improve with the intent on achieving your goal.

Professionalism: Treat coworkers and our student customers with the same level of respect you expect from them. Be courteous, supportive, reliable, attentive, and responsible. Accept all others for who they are. Be inclusive. Carry yourself in the most upright and ethical manner and expect no less from those whom you engage.

OK, so maybe that's a little bit longer than "Rowing the Boat," but I felt the need to expound on the description. These are more than just words; they are a foundation of culture. Using the student-focused enrollment SOP program mantra provided my organization with a building block and a sense of unity. I delivered a message that provided an opportunity for people to be better people, proud of what they do for a living; better people, understanding their responsibility to perform for the sake of the team and organization; better coworkers, respectful and appreciative of each other, bonded together pursuing a common goal: to deliver exceptional service for our student customers.

Those who took it to heart certainly had a worthwhile work experience, whether they were part of the team for a short term or if they were there for the long haul. They lived the SOP and presented themselves throughout the organization in that manner on a regularly consistent basis. It paid off. Those who didn't "buy in" did just that—they didn't—and they didn't last in the organization: unwilling and unable...and unemployed. See you later; thanks for playing. Having a program mantra provided a rallying point and commonality for my organization which grew to nearly one thousand coworkers in six different offices in three states at its peak in 2010. It provided unity, clarity, and direction and helped us win.

Coach Fleck carried the program mantra and message of unity to the University of Minnesota when he was hired as head coach in 2017. His first year at the helm was nothing to write home about, as the team delivered a 5–7 record and missed playing in a bowl game. However, things turned around in 2018, as Coach Fleck was able to bring in a good recruiting class, finishing the season with a 7–6 record while winning the Quick Lane Bowl over Georgia Tech. Rowing the Boat took hold again. The stage was set for a big 2019, and Coach Fleck and the Golden Gophers delivered.

They started the season with nine consecutive wins, which hadn't happened for the University of Minnesota football program since 1904, including a win over then-ranked number 4 Penn State. Even with a couple of bumps in the road, the team finished the regular season at 10–2 and were scheduled to play Auburn University in the Outback Bowl. Coach Fleck signed a seven-year contract in November; the Golden Gophers football program became relevant once again much in part due to Coach Fleck. He won the coaches' vote for Big Ten Coach of the Year, and expectations are high for the 2020 program.

But best of all, at least as it pertains to me and the importance of having a program mantra, was what occurred as I watched the Outback Bowl on January 1, 2020. I was pulling for UM and Coach Fleck. This was a big opportunity for him and his team to gain credibility, make believers out of the doubters, and bring national attention to the program. I was excited and nervous at the same time. I hoped Coach Fleck and team could win this game. It was going to be a tough battle against a very good Auburn team from the traditional football powerhouse Southeastern Conference.

Then it happened.

The television cameras panned the crowd from a variety of different angles and when they focused on the UM side of the field, I saw it. I should have known and expected it, but it still hit me hard, and the adrenaline rush that came with it made me stand up and take note. I have no ties to the University of Minnesota or its football program, but at that moment I felt I was part of the team. I saw thousands of UM fans clad in their maroon T-shirts with the gold inscription on the front, Row THE BOAT. And I knew there was another important aspect of the program mantra brought to my attention. The fans in the stands. The supporters watching on television. The alumni. The students. The people who aren't on the field but who are part of the program mantra none the less. They live the mantra. They believe in the mantra. They are the program.

Good team or not, Auburn was playing against more than just the UM football players that day. They were playing against a new UM culture that was ingrained and very much alive and thriving in the commitment from those engaged in the UM football program.

Final score University of Minnesota 31, Auburn University 24.

UM completed a solid season ranked at number 10 in the AP Poll. I'll bet Coach Fleck was happy, but not satisfied. I'll bet he has his sights set on continuous improvement, perhaps a Big Ten title and another big bowl game victory. But one thing at a time. Let's not look too far ahead. The old cliché of playing them one at a time is absolutely correct. I don't know if Coach Fleck will look back on 2019 as motivation for 2020, but I do know this. The message he delivers to have a successful 2020 will be clear, loud, and omnipresent: Row The Boat.

And I'm going to buy a T-shirt.

LESSON 3: LEARN SOMETHING FROM EVERYONE; TEACH THOSE WHO WILL LISTEN

You don't send the puppy dog in to clean up the puppy dog's mess.
—Harvey Specter in the television series *Suits*

During my downtime from sales training, working as a vice president of enrollment, writing this book, spending time with the family, which includes enjoying my duties as a grandpa to Bastian or going to the casino when the opportunity presents itself (there are no casinos in Texas, so perhaps that's a good thing), my wife, Robin, and I enjoy binge-watching television programs. We got into this late-night activity when Robin's daughter Carin sent us the complete DVD set of the television series *Mr. Selfridge* for a Christmas gift. I was a little skeptical at first since I'm more of a moviegoer than a series-watching kind of guy, but I figured I might as well give it a chance. Not much to lose but a few hours of sleep anyway, so what the heck. I was soon hooked. What a great way to wind down from a stressed day by spending a couple of hours or so watching commercial-free soap opera drama. _Mr. Selfridge_ starred Jeremy Piven and offered a complete escape from current reality yet provided a glimpse into what may have been actual retail business practices during the early 1900s. I thoroughly enjoyed the series and wanted more.

We moved on to a variety of series, thanks to Amazon Prime and Netflix and now Disney + and binge-watched as often as we could. We spent time in the Los Angeles police department with homicide detective Harry Bosch in _Bosch,_ in New York and New Jersey with Mafia crime boss Tony Soprano and his family in _The Sopranos,_ and in the backwoods of Kentucky with US marshal Raylan Givens in _Justified_. (I highly recommend all three series if you haven't already watched.) _Boardwalk Empire_, _Ozark_, _Game of Thrones_ (I only binge-watched; it was not Robin's kind of show), _The Crown_, _Longmire_, among many others, all made the binge-watch list with pleasurable results. My new favorite is _The Mandalorian_, and I am looking forward to season two when released.

We even watched _Downton Abbey_. I liked it so much that I went with Robin to see the movie! Stop laughing. I'm a true softie at heart when it comes to soap opera drama mixed in with a little bit of history, sexual innuendo, and devious subplots. Again, my enjoyment in this regard centers around binge-watching what allows for an escape from reality without reading too much into the story lines. Just enjoy the show for entertainment value. Try not to relate the episode plots to any real-life situations. Avoid any glaring comparisons between the characters and people you know including yourself. Get away from the work strife. Just enjoy. Just relax. Just escape.

Then we watched *Suits*.

My perspective and everything associated with, related to, or in any way comparable in the least bit to what I learned and proclaim to know about being a role model and a mentor all changed in minutes, thanks to *Suits'* lead character, Harvey Specter. With high-powered attorney Harvey Specter, the word *mentor* takes on a whole new meaning, like jalapeño provides an awakening flavor to a taco. The difference is stunning, dramatic, refreshing, and extenuated while, at the same time, it becomes relevant to a routine dining experience. I'm sure comparing Harvey Specter to a jalapeño pepper is perhaps putting it mildly...pardon the pun. Harvey Specter, or at least the character portrayed by actor Gabriel Macht, is anything but bland. He is hot in more ways than one. He is egotistical, treacherous, bold, stunning, and creative. His arrogance is outweighed only by his vanity. His cockiness and confidence hold no boundaries. He backs up his persona by being intelligent to an extreme and outwits, outpuzzles, and outmatches all opponents in any and all situations. He is the modern-day attorney version of an arrogant Sherlock Holmes—simply better than all challengers because he is smarter than all challengers—and he lets it be known.

"Sorry, I can't hear you over the sound of how awesome I am"— is one quote from Harvey Specter. Evidence presented.

Summary statement: There is nothing about Harvey Specter's intelligence level that he doesn't allow to be witnessed.

I do not have a man-crush on Harvey Specter. I simply admire his ability to outthink everybody else. That is a very attractive quality. Think what you may. And then remind yourself of how many times you wished you could be the smartest person in the room. Maybe you are most times, but for regular guys like me, Harvey Specter represents an icon of intelligence, easily identified and admired, annoyed and frustrating at the same time. I want to be like Harvey Specter in some ways, but I don't want to be like Harvey Specter in others.

For those not familiar with _Suits_, here's a brief synopsis. _Suits_ is a legal drama/comedy series that centers around Harvey and his protégé, Mike Ross, portrayed by actor Patrick J. Adams. Harvey has just been promoted to senior partner at the fictional firm Pearson–Hardman. With that comes the responsibility of hiring a new associate attorney for the firm, which only hires Harvard Law School graduates. By chance, Mike stumbles into the interview hiring process, as he is fleeing from the police who suspect him of carrying a briefcase of drugs—which he is, as the "mule" for his friend in lieu of a $25,000 delivery payment. Mike impresses Harvey with his knowledge of the law and how he outwitted the police and gained access to the interview. Mike is currently earning money by taking the Law School Admission Test, LSAT for others, helping them cheat their way into law school. Harvey wants to hire Mike on the spot, not because he's a cheat, but because of his uncanny ability to memorize what he reads and understands and is a walking encyclopedia of the law. However, there is only one problem. Mike is a college dropout— no undergraduate degree, and obviously no Harvard Law School degree. Harvey hires Mike anyway, recognizing Mike's potential and talent for the law, placing his own integrity on the line and with the intent to cover up Mike's lack of paper trail. From that point on, _Suits_ is a series of law cases, drama, comedy and competition between Harvey and countless foils, with the underlying story revolving around how smart Mike is and how, together, they must protect his secret from all interested parties, or else they will both get fired. Or else Mike goes to jail, and Harvey's career is ruined. Or else there is no television show.

Oh, and there's also the story of Harvey mentoring Mike and Mike's constant badgering of the omnipotent Harvey. Harvey presents himself as bulletproof, but Mike believes beneath all that armor plating is someone who cares—a key element of a mentor.

By pure definition, a mentor is a trustworthy person of influence and advising who cares about you and your development. This very well could be a peer or even someone outside of your company. The mentor serves as a support person providing valuable input in a variety of areas, with the common theme of having your best interests in mind. The right mentor asks what they can do for you and is one who places your needs above their own. The right mentor shares their knowledge and expertise without hesitation. The right mentor is a role model who always acts with complete integrity. There is a sense of trust between mentor and mentee that unifies and bonds the relationship to a unique level; it can't and won't be broken.

Which brings me back to Harvey Specter.

Person of influence: check.

Person of integrity: uncheck.

Person of trust: sometimes.

How can Harvey Specter be such a great mentor if he is so wrapped up in himself, his outcomes, his own best interests, if he can't be trusted and operates outside the lines of complete integrity? He's not a crooked lawyer. He just manipulates situations for his own best interests. He does not lie. He will not commit perjury. Yet he is hiding a secret regarding Mike's lack of formal education. He asks Mike to trust him throughout the series. Mike wants to learn as much as possible from Harvey, yet he wants to break the bond of trust by coming clean about not having a formal degree. What a mess. But there is hope.

I believe I have myself stumbled across the answer to the conundrum. It's only a television series, right? Well, maybe so, but the fact remains that not all mentor-mentee situations are perfect, and *Suits* provides us with an example that underscores the subject of this lesson: Learn Something from Everyone and Teach Those Who Will Listen.

Life isn't perfect. People aren't perfect. And those two premises are entertainingly portrayed in *Suits* by Harvey and Mike as an example of reality. With all its twists, turns, and subplots, the thing I keep coming back to in _Suits_ is Mike's hunger to learn from Harvey, and Harvey's ultimate desire to win, always. This is very similar to a sales manager mentor – sales representative mentee relationship. Mike is the mentee, with a fresh approach to problems; he is willing to push back to his mentor, Harvey, and is not a yes man. He is fighting for his own place in the firm, his life, and in relationships. Harvey, however, presses on as the badass he is, taking on and taking out all foes with confidence, cunning, arrogance, and tenacity in his role as the best closer in the firm…and in Harvey's mind, of any firm, anywhere.

Throughout my career in sales management, I experienced working with people who want to learn and those who want to teach. But I've also come across many people who want neither. Not to say they are bad people, but they just don't have the appetite to take on the responsibility that comes with being a teacher or mentor, nor do they care to gain any further knowledge to assist in their own advancement professionally or academically. They just seem to exist. Just floating along. No real course of direction or desire. Just there. Easy to ignore, bypass, overlook, and overrun. But also, they are very easy to learn from in the sense that they provide information and understanding about the day-to-day course of business that those at the top simply assume.

I've observed in many of these individuals they don't seem to mind that they're not on anybody's radar or on the fast track to being promoted. They're satisfied. They're happy. They've accepted their circumstances and not only learned to live within their expectations, but they are enjoying themselves in doing so.

To that I say, if that's what does it for you, then OK by me. There's no lesson in this book about force-feeding someone who doesn't want to be taught anything outside of what they know and certainly no direction that mandates you to mentor. I know what worked for me and have come to realize that there are lessons learned in what works for others.

All I'm saying here is that I found success in taking the time to try to learn from as many people as I could, that everyone I met or worked with had something to offer if I looked for it. Perhaps they were content with their career aspirations, but that didn't mean I couldn't learn something from them. A mentor doesn't always have to be a person above you on the food chain. A mentor can be anyone who provides you the opportunity to learn something about yourself as well. And I've found that quite a bit of what I learned along the sales management way came from those who did the day-to-day work, not those who ran the operation.

I read somewhere a long time ago that you don't have to be nice to people on the way up if you don't plan on going back down again in the future. What a crock. Those that live by that unfortunate premise don't have a clue. I say just the opposite. Be a person who appreciates others and take the time to learn from any and all, as I firmly believe everyone has something to offer, both good and perhaps not so good, but certainly worth learning.

Make this premise a way of your daily thinking. *Everyone has something of value to offer.*

Which, once again, brings me back to Harvey Specter. Upon further observation, I concur with Mike that underneath Harvey's hardcore persona is a relatively appreciative, caring person. He just doesn't want to be perceived as soft; it would go against everything he is supposed to represent as being the omnipotent winner-take-all closer. He represents the firm and, in doing so, has an image to portray. Opposition attorneys must see him as an insurmountable challenge not only because of his superior intellect, but also because of his larger than life persona.

But Mike knows Harvey better than everyone—at least, almost better than everyone. Only Harvey's faithful assistant Donna Paulsen, portrayed by Sarah Rafferty, has an equal if not better handle on Harvey than Mike. If you want something from Harvey, you best be on Donna's good side. She is Harvey's rock. Together, Mike and Donna both see a side of Harvey that offers a profound characteristic of a true mentor: Harvey has their collective backs. As they say in the military, Harvey has the six. He is watching out for them in any and all situations. Perhaps for his own best interests—he needs both Mike and Donna to support his own success—but for all intents and purposes, Harvey wants Mike and Donna to succeed as well. He needs them as much as they need him.

He covers for them when there are challenges from others. In public, he touts their uncanny abilities and superior results to others ("It's not bragging if it's true") and supports their career development. He protects their errors in judgment, criticizes their shortcomings, and challenges their thinking when it is not as intelligent as his, and he does so privately with tough-love encouragement. He is the epitome of a character who will do what it takes to ensure their loyalty. And that loyalty is well earned. Harvey is respected and admired for who he is to Mike and Donna, more so than what he does as the closer. He is their confidant. He is their go-to guy. He is their trusted advisor. He is Harvey Specter; the attorney other lawyers hope to emulate because they only see the outer shell of the man. But to Mike and Donna, he is far more than just an attorney. They see Harvey as their leader. For Mike and Donna, loyalty to Harvey comes relatively easily. With all his shortcomings, Harvey has earned their respect and trust and thereby their loyalty. They believe him and in him.

Harvey is the television-character version of the subject matter of this lesson learned. He truly is an example of a person who determined that learning something from everyone, whether good or bad, is still learning, and built his superior intellect on that premise. He knows what to do as often as he knows what not to do, based on his understanding and experience in dealing with people. He recognizes that in teaching Mike and Donna, and learning from them as well, he is protecting himself, his operation, his legitimacy, and his career success. But he is also developing long lasting and sincere relationships, another characteristic of being a true mentor.

So, sales managers, if you watched _Suits_ and came away with a similar perspective of Harvey Specter and his team, well, maybe then we are on the same page. For those of you who watched _Suits_ but didn't come to that conclusion regarding Harvey, well, maybe you will watch again to verify your first thoughts and confirm your disagreement. For those of you who haven't watched _Suits_, please do so, and draw your own conclusions regarding Harvey as a likely mentor. The real challenge you will have is in watching _Suits_ only as entertainment value. Just a television show. Just relaxation. Just an escape. I believe you will be challenged to try not to identify with any real-life mentoring situations.

Suits offers characters with strong personalities and there are obvious additional opportunities to observe a mentor – mentee relationship outside of the Harvey – Mike relationship. Yet, this is the one that resonates the most with me as a sales manager. It's not perfect. This mentor – mentee relationship is volatile, challenging, argumentative, judgmental, and respectful all at the same time. Above all, it's realistic.

LESSON 4: COACH TO MOTIVATE: RECOGNIZE THE INDIVIDUAL NEED

He who has no fire in himself cannot warm others.

One of the greatest aspects about being a parent is the opportunity to be involved in your child's growth and development during their formative years. Believe me, there is no greater feeling than watching your little mini-me(s) become self-aware, communicate, learn, take on challenges, laugh, cry, and basically just plain experience life. Yes, while they are individuals with their own personas, you can't help but think, "I had something to do with that, I helped create that, I helped mold that person." It really is up to them to determine their direction in life, and as a parent, the only thing you can do is provide a stimulus to guide them in a certain direction.

I told myself to provide my kids options. Let them experience a variety of different things to encourage them to choose what they liked to do and be there if they needed a little "opinion."

(I learned long ago not to give advice. I'll give you my opinion, but advice is way too personal, direct, and concrete, and it carries a stigma of expertise along with blame if things don't work out. My "opinion" is more about what I think I would do in your situation, carries less accountability, and avoids blame if things don't work out. The real decision-making choice is going to be yours, not mine.)

In being a father to my children, I tried as best as possible to live by this mantra. Life is all about choices and making good choices will be the premise by which they will be guided.

Except when it comes to ice hockey.

Or in actual terms when it came to whether my older son, Christopher, was going to play ice hockey. He started ice skating at age two—I have the picture to prove it—and he was going to take after me and play ice hockey. No choices, no options, no outside influences.

My wife was on board when she saw Christopher skate at age five, as we did the father-son skates on Sundays at "Rocky Hockey," conducted by former National Hockey League professional player Rocky Saganiuk. Rocky held a skate every Sunday for the little guys and gals who were not quite ready to be Mites, which at that time was limited to seven-, eight-, and nine-year-olds, so Rocky Hockey provided an opportunity for five- and six-year-olds to put on full equipment and experience skate-arounds. Just a few moms and dads with thirty or so pre-Mites, having fun skating and learning some fundamentals, like how to stop, fall safely, get up correctly, take good strides, things like that. Christopher was good on skates, he enjoyed it, and I certainly felt a pride in knowing he took to the sport that I love so much.

Then it happened. As he progressed and made a Gold Mite Team, my wife said to me, "You know, you should coach. Maybe get your own team next year." That's all I needed to hear. I did not need any further motivation other than her permission. I completed and submitted my USA Hockey coaching certification application, went to the necessary clinics, got my coach's card, and became a Gold Mite Coach. I was going to be an ice hockey coach for seven-, eight- and nine-year-old Mites!

As it turned out, I was able to coach my son for the next seven years until he went on to high school and play four years of high school hockey. Yes, he could skate; he won the fastest skater competition at a tournament skills competition when he was a senior in high school. All the emphasis on the basics of skating certainly paid off for him. As far as motivating him to compete, the only stimulus I ever had to provide Christopher to prove he was the fastest player on the ice was to tell him there was someone on the other team with a tagline, "They say he's faster than you." Done deal. That's all it took. He was good to go. No one could touch him at his playing level when it came to straight speed up and down the ice. That speed came in handy quite often, as Christopher's best role on the high school varsity team was to kill penalties, scoring several short-handed goals in the process throughout his career.

And with that said, here comes the lesson learned about motivation being an individualized process.

Through those seven years of coaching ice hockey players from Mites to Bantams, I was able to keep a core group of players together. While there were always a few new additions to the team as families moved in and out of the area and kids dropped out of competitive hockey, I became close to parents and their children— players who were on my team every year. And hence the motivation lesson: I learned what I needed to do to prompt my core group of kids to deliver at their maximum effort. We didn't win every game. But we won a lot. Best of all, we played as a team. I didn't need to provide a stimulus to the kids to get them to appreciate their teammates. I did need to provide a stimulus to get them to maximize their abilities. They wanted to play because they were engaged in a competitive sport and experienced the gratification that comes along with delivering a solid effort, and ultimately winning.

However, I didn't coach winning with my teams, although I certainly wanted to win every game. I coached to put forth effort, develop hockey skill sets, learn to respect the game and the competition, and most importantly, to have fun. Those four variables are much more important to a youngster's development than to completely focus on winning every game (note to parents).

But in order to get each player to fully enjoy their hockey experience, I needed to know what stimulus to provide for each player. When you're talking about eight-year-olds, the variables are incredibly personalized.

My son's friend, also named Chris, wanted to know that he was in the starting lineup each game; that's all it took to get him ready and willing. He just wanted to be one of the first five skaters plus our goalie on the ice as the game started. (He was my son Chris's defense partner, and he was certainly good enough to be in the starting lineup, so no issues from me at all.) Eric wanted to be sure he could be on a forward line with his friends from school. John wanted to be the first one out of the locker room and on the ice after our goalie, Brian, led the team out of the locker room. Chuck had to be the last one out of the locker room, right before me and the assistant coach, his dad, Bill. Mike needed me to pull him aside before each game and tell him how much I appreciated him looking out for his teammates, that he was a player his teammates looked up to. Patrick wanted to be the one to lead the team cheer in the locker room prior to the game. Kevin had to be the one who took the first shot on goal in the pregame warmup. And on and on and on and on. All little quirks, but all important to each of the individuals on my teams.

While I ensured a pregame ritual, most important, however, is what I did after every game. Once we were back in the locker room after the game had ended, I went player by player and said something positive to each of my players. It didn't matter what the score of the game ended up being or what errors occurred during the game; this moment was all positive reinforcement. All about providing an individualized stimulus to motivate these youngsters to want to come back for tomorrow night's practice and look forward to getting back on the ice.

Jeez, I loved coaching hockey! I loved what I learned, what I was able to teach, and how the relationship between providing a stimulus to a young hockey player was not much different than providing a stimulus to a seasoned sales representative to enjoy their job and deliver results.

So, being that I am long retired from coaching ice hockey players, and recently retired from coaching sales managers and their teams, I can't help but find myself in situations whereby I am reminded about motivation in the workplace.

I'm not in the habit of eavesdropping on conversations, but while enjoying lunch a few days ago, I heard this statement from the conversation at the next table: "I just don't know what motivates them." Yikes! Further listening provided me with information that person A, who made the statement, was the sales manager, and person B was the marketing director for this not-to-be-named company. The marketing director mostly listened and only offered a few "I understand what you're going through" and a couple of "I hear what you're saying" comments while generally being empathetic and not offering any solution to the situation.

I wanted to jump in. I wanted to immediately go into sales management ice hockey coaching training mode and help the sales manager solve her issue. I wanted to but realized without having all the information and full understanding of the individuals and the situation from both sides of the equation, I may be doing more harm than good. I returned to my rueben sandwich and kept my thoughts to myself.

· And here are those thoughts:

Pardon me for hearing your conversation, but you should consider putting all further conversations on hold and get out the Sales Management 101 training guide. There you will discover that motivation is a key element in the sales manager's mantra of success. Turn to the part about a sales manager providing a positive stimulus to be able to influence others. Read this and take this premise to the bank: *to be successful in leading people, a sales manager must learn, understand, and know what motivates individual team members in order to influence those people to deliver desired results. Once knowledge is gained, the sales manager must then provide the correct stimulus to influence the individual sales representative to be motivated. This process must be repeated, updated, and reinforced on a regular basis.*

If you are having difficulty in determining what motivates your sales staff, allow me the opportunity to guide you through some quick but valuable options to tackle this issue. First, however, you must do two things to ensure your commitment to engage in this valuable sales management premise.

Old-school sales managers:

Step 1: Write down the italicized premise from the above paragraph on a large Post-it note, and stick that note to your desktop or laptop, or whatever you would consider your workstation.

Step 2: Do something with this note that allows

you the opportunity to see it repeatedly until you get the concept down by demonstrating it daily with your team.

New-school sales managers:
Step 1: Make a note for yourself in your cell phone.
Then follow step 2 as listed above.

Ultra-new-school sales managers:
Step 1: Create notes in your Surface Pro or iPad.
Then follow Step 2 as listed above.

Now that you're committed to figuring out your team's individual motivations, let's gain a basic understanding of stimulus: motivation.

I am a firm believer that all motivation is internal. I can influence you, but the real motivation to get something done comes from what you determine is important. So, therefore, it is essential that the sales manager understand what motivates a person on the team.

Motivation is, by pure definition, an individual's desire to put forth the effort required to meet a need.

There are a variety of factors that can be possible motivational influences on salespeople. These factors can include financial rewards, nonfinancial rewards, and job-specific rewards.

What motivates an individual is best defined by that individual. Those motivations, when successfully defined for the individual salesperson, and properly implemented by the sales manager, can be a foundation for a happy and well-appreciated salesperson who desires to perform at the appropriate expected level.

But the real question is this: "How do I know what motivates my sales representatives?"

Many of you right now just answered the question to yourself in this manner: "Just ask them." And while that direct approach may yield a measure of results, it may not provide you with the underlying details you need to fully understand each person's personal motivations. I would wager that if you ask the sales team what motivates them, you will get the standard answers: money, recognition, sense of accomplishment, opportunity for advancement, sense of pride in doing a good job, and being accepted as part of the team, among others. Fear may provide a stimulus to motivate a person. However, I believe fear is a short-term motivation tactic, not a very good one at that, and is not to be considered a standard operating procedure for a people-first, results oriented sales manager or people-focused organization, for that matter. No one really wants to be in a position wherein they fear for their job based on a sales manager reminding them constantly about what could happen if they don't produce. Fear as a motivation stimulus leads to lack of respect and high turnover. Yet when answering the question, fear or fear of failure normally comes up as one of the motivation factors.

What's listed above are good answers but can be construed as generic. Have you ever worked with any salesperson who is worth her measure who didn't want to receive appropriate compensation, be recognized for doing her job, or take personal pride in her work and accomplishments? Perhaps she is on the fast track for promotion. Perhaps she is highly competitive by nature and needs to win every sales contest as a matter of personal satisfaction. Perhaps the loyalty to the organization is enough of a motivating factor to have her exceed sales expectations.

Just a brief side comment on whether money is a motivator: a good compensation package considers more than just the monetary reward. I've reviewed numerous studies that indicate that money is not necessarily the number-one motivational factor for a salesperson. Salespeople, just like those in any other profession, expect to be fairly compensated for their efforts and results.

So how do I determine what motivates my sales team? Here's an exercise I used to do that helped my new sales managers understand the answer to this vital question.

I had the pleasure of working with many first-time sales managers, recently promoted to new levels of responsibility. I made it a point to meet with those new managers on a one-on-one basis after their promotion or if they were hired into our organization as a manager. Then I would meet with them after a few months on the job. One of our topics of discussion was their direct reports, their sales team, and what individual characteristics each member brought to the table. Basically, I wanted the manager to tell me what he thought was each member's personal motivation. I would sometimes ask the manager to prepare a one-page document prior to our meeting and list the motivation factors for each team member for us to discuss at our meeting. I asked the manager not to discuss with the team, just to come to the meeting prepared with what they thought was each member's motivation factors.

Now this may be a bit under the table but, unbeknownst to the manager, I had already been in communication with each of the team members. I let them know I was in a coaching scenario with their manager and asked them to keep my request private for now. I asked them to provide me a paragraph about their personal motivations. It was like the answer above ("just ask them"), but keep in mind this request was from several levels up in the managerial rank, not from their direct manager. By letting them know I was interested in them and cared about their well-being on the job, and they knew I was a straight shooter; they trusted me. They knew this information would be used to help them, not hurt them.

Much of the information I gathered was more specific to each person's own situation. Along with the generic motivation factors listed, several people told me they were working to make their family proud. Yes, earning the money was important to pay the bills, but knowing that they were providing for their family and the satisfaction they received from that knowledge was a much more significant motivation factor than the money itself.

Several people told me they were saving for their children's college and wanted them to be debt free when they attended. That is a huge task, certainly worthy of providing a motivation stimulus. Others talked about their team status, personal well-being, competitiveness with friends and coworkers, and the desire to be successful, itself personally defined. A few talked about Mom and Dad, brothers and sisters, and those who believed in them.

Here's the one that stuck with me the most: *others talked about those who placed a limit on them in a prior establishment and how that negative experience was all the motivation they needed to prove they could and would do the job.* You know how that works on people when told they can't do something? They're not good enough, they're too small, they don't have the right makeup, not the right fit, they'll never get promoted, and so on.

I love having those people on my team. They have something to prove. They are fighters! They are winners! Their motivation is already engrained in their personal makeup.

To answer the question in simple terms, the best way to find out what stimulus you need to provide to your individual sales representatives in order to motivate them, you must be able to build a relationship with them to gain their confidence, their trust, and their willingness to open up about their individual situations. This information will prove invaluable. You will know what and why, and they will know you have a genuine interest in their well-being. That is the ultimate foundation for providing a stimulus for personal motivation.

I would share and compare notes with the sales manager in our one-on-one discussion, and most times, what the manager thought were the individual motivation factors were a lot different from what information I had gathered. But not to worry—this exercise was all taken in a positive manner designed to assist the manager, help the team, and keep me involved with my management organization.

One other thing that is critical and not to be overlooked is the team aspect of motivation. When you and your sales representatives build a relationship of mutual respect and trust, don't be afraid to tell them what motivates you—and do it in a team setting. Get your team together, face to face if possible, and let them know how much you appreciate their effort, their competitiveness, their intent on winning, their drive to be successful, and how those factors play into motivating you to be the best sales manager you can possibly be.

That team approach certainly worked for me in coaching hockey. I remember a playoff game where my team was the clear-cut underdog. We made the playoffs but were up against the top-rated team from the northern suburbs of Chicago. They were flat-out better than every other team in our league. They beat us earlier in the year in the regular season, and it was evident they expected to win all the time. They were coached that way. Always win. They didn't really know how to lose. So, prior to this playoff game, I told myself I had an opportunity to use that against them.

We would go through the standard pregame ritual for each player; however, this time, I did something a little different. Before we left the locker room, I put all the players on one side of the room so I could see each of their faces while I talked to them. I told them how proud I was of what they did as a team through the year. I told them they were a great bunch of kids to coach and how much fun we had throughout the year. Then I told them that today's game was going to be the hardest game they've ever had to play in their young hockey careers. That the team on the other end of the rink was supposedly the best in the league. That no one outside of this locker room—not even their parents—believed we had a chance today. (Oh, God forgive me for bringing up their parents in that manner.)

Then I told them that I believed, and the other coaches believed, and that as a team, we believed in each other. That when we get on the ice, we have an opportunity to prove everyone else in the rink is wrong. That we know better and that we can and will win this game, and we will do it because we play as a team. That they won't know what hit them when we get out of this locker room. That those nonbelievers will see something they've never seen before from us today.

This was the perfect time to coach winning, and I took total advantage of the scenario. These kids had a reason to be motivated; together they had a common purpose. Together, they had a self-ingrained stimulus. They were told that other people, even their parents, didn't believe they could compete with the best. They had something to prove as a team.

To this day, I regret I told them their parents didn't believe they could win. I didn't say their parents didn't believe in them, just that they didn't think we could win against such a stacked opponent.

We won 2–1.

LESSON 5: PROSPECT WITH PURPOSE: FISH WHERE THE FISH ARE

Pray for a good harvest but continue to hoe.

This past summer provided me with an opportunity that I hadn't experienced in nearly thirty years. I went fishing. Not just pond fishing, but real fishing, walleye fishing, northern pike fishing, the way I remember it to be. In Canada.

Growing up in Chicago, I was fortunate enough to have a family who loved to fish—or, at least, they wanted to get out of the city and breathe some fresh air. It just so happened that our next-door neighbor owned a fishing resort in Sioux Lookout, Ontario, Canada. So nearly every summer, we would pack up the car, and drive eight hundred miles north to spend a week in the woods, roughing it.

At that time, the "resort" had no running water—no hot water, for that matter, unless you boiled your own on the makeshift burner—no indoor restroom facilities, and no electricity. For heat, there was a log-burning stove in the middle of the cabin.

You washed in the lake or filled a bucket with water from the water tank to wash up in the sink in the cabin. Lake water, unfiltered, was readily available for drinking, straight from Vermillion Lake. My dad would scoop a glass of water and drink it while we were fishing. Maybe that's why he had stomach problems later in life. No such thing as bottled water at that time, so I stuck to canned soda from the grocery store.

Coleman lanterns provided the light in the cabin. You lit a match, turned the knob on the lantern to release the kerosene vapor, and held the lit match inside the glass lantern close to the mantle webbing, but not too close to burn a hole in the webbing. Of course, being only eight years old the first time I lit a lantern, I burned right through the webbing, which provided a loud "pop" and a bit of embarrassment. Anybody could do that. The trick was to just get enough of a kerosene vapor flow and allow the match to do the work. A little practice and it worked fine. I became proficient and was the lamp lighter for the cabin.

The "facility" (the outhouse) was located a short walk from the cabin. My biggest fear about using the outhouse was wondering if I would happen to come across a bear that may have wandered into camp looking for food. You didn't dare go out of the cabin after dark unless it was an absolute necessity. Grab the flashlight, scan the woods from inside the cabin screen door, run to the outhouse, make sure no one was currently in there, lock the door (which meant latching the hook-and-eye latch, requiring the flashlight to see the latch), check the wood bench and hole for creatures, business done promptly, open the door, scan the woods again, flashlight in hand run as fast as possible back to the cabin…and hope your older brother didn't lock you out so as to afford you the opportunity to fully experience the Canadian darkness in the woods at its finest, scariest moments. Love the Canadian lake vacations, but there was just one little problem.

The thing about Vermillion Lake, where the resort was located, was that it wasn't a walleye lake. There were some northern pike and bass, but mostly it was a trout lake. Fishing for trout is grueling in the summer, or any time, for that matter. The reason being that during the summer months, they are comfortable at fifty to sixty feet of water, which meant letting out a lot of line. In those days, wire line was on a huge reel, which had a six-inch silver spoon attached as bait. The hard part was learning to get a feel for a fish at a challenging water depth. There were no fish finders or depth finders at that time, or at least we didn't have one. We had to fish by feel. Very challenging. Very boring! I never caught a lake trout. It was nice to be out on the water but come on. Fishing is only fun when you are catching fish!

So, in order to enjoy our Canadian fishing adventures, we traveled from the resort via car on dirt roads to other lakes in the vicinity where our neighbor had stored (chained and locked to a tree) a boat or two and fished the lakes in which walleye were prevalent. My first-ever airplane flight was on a fly-in to a lake that was not necessarily navigable by car. We portaged from one lake to another; that meant getting to a part of a lake that required you to carry the boat and motor and all the gear through the woods. It was a simply wonderful experience when you have your hands full and mosquitos are lunching on your exposed neck. I wouldn't trade those memories. It was all part of roughing it and learning to survive in the deep woods. Most importantly, it was required to catch walleye. We knew we would catch walleye a-plenty because we knew the lakes and the spots on those lakes where walleye were in abundance. If you've never eaten a walleye, caught moments earlier fresh from the lake and pan fried for shore lunch, it is perhaps one of the greatest culinary experiences that you are missing. Real fishermen and women will go to great lengths to overcome challenges to obtain their goals: catch fish, especially the best eating fish in the world, pan-fried walleye.

To that point here's the lesson learned: Fish Where the Fish Are!

Seems simple enough, right? Yet it requires experience, knowledge, the right equipment, patience, and persistence among other things. It's very similar to sales, wouldn't you agree?

A major emphasis in sales is the need to pursue new business. In order to keep the profitable revenue coming in and to obtain sales growth goals, the selling team must deliver an increase in business. This is expected year over year—quarter over quarter, in some instances, and month over month in others. The sales manager is at the core of the expectation. Sustainable growth requires a consistent and properly executed sales prospecting strategy.

In that regard, the sales manager owns the process of mapping out the strategy to increase sales. This strategy could be based on expansion of current product or service distribution territory, increased orders from current customers, landing new customers in existing territories, taking business away from the competition, buying out the competition, adding new products or services to sell, and perhaps improving online options to supplement current product or service sales.

Same question asked previously. All the sales manager needs to do is analyze all those abovementioned options and factor in the experience, knowledge, product or service for sale relative to market demand, have a great advertising program and lead generation commitment from marketing, and voilà! Sales increase automatically.

Yep, you might as well just get in a boat on Vermillion Lake and try to catch a walleye. There's no difference, because the one key ingredient to all the planning and prep work that goes into designing a sales strategy is missing. Selling to those who want to buy your product means that you know who and where those potential customers operate. The key element is to know the marketplace and in turn knowing what your product or service will sell for in that marketplace. Effectively, you are prospecting for customers who want what you are selling.

You are fishing where the fish are!

Too often, and too recently, I was associated with individuals who had no understanding of this basic premise. They were under the impression that the service we offered was so well worth it that we should be attracting customers from across the country. Our price point didn't matter. What mattered was the historical tradition of our service. The reputation, which had been severely damaged over the years, and the outcomes from those that were able to take full advantage of the service was supposedly enough to sell the service.

Oh, how they missed the mark. They refused to invest in market research to understand the marketplace, and in so doing, they failed to identify and acknowledge the reality in the marketplace: an overpriced service with a declining poor reputation, no viable advertising exposure (I am a firm believer that all the best advertising in the world can't sell a bad product, so I'll go easy on this aspect), no new products to roll out, no physical improvements to the facilities (a key selling point ignored), consistently being outperformed by the competition in our own backyard, no opportunity for expansion in key markets, and no online offerings.

The expectation was growth without support. Growth without acknowledging and correcting the key barriers to increase sales. Growth without a clue as to where to fish. This provided just another lesson learned in my forty-plus years of sales and sales management. *Prospecting with a purpose requires an understanding of the marketplace and the support to execute a sales strategy designed to turn prospects into customers.* The first step in turning prospects into customers is to identify the right prospects by knowing who and where they are located. The second step is to know what they will purchase, and most importantly, is to make a complete commitment to the premise that they will purchase for their reasons, not yours.

While the methods of how prospecting with purpose may have changed over the years with the ability to learn the market via online options, the concept of identifying those qualified prospects who have the likeliness to turn into customers has not changed at all. To get customers, you must know where to prospect. To catch fish, you must fish where the fish are!

How things with fishing have changed over the years as well. My brother Ken invited me to join him and his son Ken Jr. (my nephew) and his son Jack (my great-nephew) for a week at Temple Bay Lodge, Eagle Lake Ontario. He had asked me several times before to join in on the trip, but I was always too distracted, away on another vacation, or working, or just too busy utilizing my vacation time for more luxurious options, like cruising the Caribbean (where the cruise ship always had plenty of running water, among other pleasantries). But this time, I said yes, let's go! I'd seen the pictures, heard the stories, knew the facilities had changed, and determined it was about time I enjoyed a "different" vacation.

Armed with what I thought to be the right equipment (later in the week, I ended up using the fishing guide's extra rod and reel—that's how poorly prepared I was), I ventured back to Canada to relive my childhood memories.

Much to my pleasure, I found very comfortable cabins equipped with running water, both hot and cold, electricity that supplied the overhead lights, refrigerator, and an in-cabin hot-water tank. Hot breakfast was ordered from the menu each morning between 6:00 and 7:00 a.m., lunch was either fresh sandwiches or walleye shore lunch, and dinner was served in the dining room between 5:30 and 6:30 p.m. Heck, they even had a bar with televisions to watch sporting events. Commissary, desserts, gift shop—this certainly wasn't "roughing it" the way I knew so many years ago; this was real resort-style fishing. Ultramodern boats with high horsepower motors, comfortable seating, fishing guides who baited your hook for you and knew just where to fish each day, and the beautiful Canadian scenery made for a truly wonderful experience.

But best of all, I was with my brother, nephew, and great-nephew, and we caught fish! I mean a lot of fish: my best was eighteen walleye in one day. Of course, we utilized catch and release and only kept our daily limit for eating and for taking home. Overall, I caught over forty-five fish in a six-day period, second only to my nephew, who caught over sixty. I also caught a 35.5-inch northern pike, the largest fish of my lifetime, but it was second to my nephew, who caught a pike that was thirty-eight inches. I was very proud of my accomplishment of coming in second place in both categories; after all, I had a variety of excuses, including a sore back, poor equipment, and a torn tendon in my right arm, which hurt consistently.

I was very proud—until my nephew reminded me that second place is just "first loser."

Yep, the Kulawiak boys, all former—and, in Jack's case, current—ice hockey players. My nephew, playing in a men's league for forty-year-old has-beens, doesn't count. We are all highly competitive by nature and certainly good at trading barbs. But you know what? I will take it for now.

Until next year, when we go back and I have more experience, knowledge, the right equipment, and the support to be successful, I will think positive and stay focused. I will compete and deliver on expectations. Of course, I will have fun. But most importantly, I'll know the method of operation and will be in a sound position to execute the strategy, with the right level of support just like in sales management.

I can't help but be successful because…I'll Fish Where the Fish Are!

LESSON 6: KNOW YOUR CRITICAL RESPONSIBILITY, AND EXECUTE ACCORDINGLY

*When you help someone up a hill, you're
that much nearer the top yourself.*

In asking sales managers to tell me about their job responsibilities and then rank those responsibilities in order of importance, the results submitted really come as no surprise.

Here's an example of what several managers provided to me:

- Hit the numbers. If we don't hit the numbers, we don't have a job.
- Be responsive to customers.
- Hire great salespeople.
- Forecast accurately.
- Build and Execute an appropriate, incentive-based compensation plan.
- Ensure positive motivation.
- Remove sales barriers. Help the team.

- Communicate effectively and concisely with the team and with the higher-ups.
- Be a servant leader.
- Make difficult decisions.

Everything on the list is worthy of being on the list. If we wanted to list ten more items, we could do it, no problem. We could debate for hours about an agreed-upon ranking of importance and most likely would not reach agreement.

Why? Because while there are numerous commonalities in which sales managers deal, there are just as many unique aspects of a business that would sway one manager to disagree with another on what is the key priority.

Do you think a sales manager at a long-haul trucking firm competing for cross-country loads with a variety of other trucking firms is faced with the same challenges as a sales manager at the local hotel who needs to fill up meeting room space and increase occupancy levels?

Perhaps there are several commonalities. Yes, they need to make the numbers. Yet the basis of their approach to earn results provides enough of a differentiator in "how" these sales managers go about their business. The process itself can be different. This alone makes each sales manager's role unique and thus impacts their opinion on the importance ranking.

However, allow me the opportunity to generalize and perhaps increase your appreciation as a sales manager for having a great team of salespeople. I am all about results through people. And I'm not talking about manipulating people for one's own advancement. I'm referring to the importance of coaching as a foundation to a salesperson's development, which, over the course of time, will deliver expected results.

If you take the position that hitting the numbers is the most critical aspect of a sales manager's job, then I applaud you for understanding the result. Yet I suggest you sharpen your focus on the process and "how" you get to the result you desire.

Numbers don't deliver themselves. People deliver numbers.

For sales managers to hit their numbers, they must spend time coaching and developing their salespeople. Have you ever heard someone say, "I don't care how you do it, just get it done"? Thanks, Coach, lots of help there. Not sure I understand why they're paying you in the first place.

Thereby a sales manager's critical responsibility that I would add to the list:

Increase ability and grow self-assurance in your salespeople. When they get better, you get better, and together you have a better chance of hitting the numbers. When you spend time guiding them to enhance their ability and develop their self-reliance, you are investing in them and their outcomes.

The process starts with people, and nothing in the sales realm occurs in a proficient manner without skilled, confident salespeople representing their company in a truly professional manner. Keep in mind I am not talking about transactional sales.

I am talking about relationship, contractual, challenging, complex long-term engagements that require people to talk to each other to reach a mutually beneficial agreement.

Think about the last time you made a major purchase. Perhaps you invested in a new car or used some of that savings account to invest in the stock market. You can do both without the help of any people!

When you do buy in that manner, the results are all on you. There is something to be said about ownership of results, but that's another lesson topic.

It is easily identifiable and apparent when working with a salesperson who has the benefit of a sales manager who takes the time to help the salesperson continue to improve in product knowledge, presentation, and personal approach to their job. You can feel it. You can see it. You can believe it. These salespeople know their stuff and are proud to represent and do so with a full capacity of confidence. You can say they were trained properly. I say they are being coached properly! Because now they are demonstrating what they learned in training with a higher level of competency and confidence!

On your next "purchase-in-person" outing, which also applies to any over the phone complex purchase, try to pay attention to the salesperson's level of competency and confidence. I guarantee you will avoid buyer's remorse in most cases when you know you just spent time with a well-coached salesperson. In fact, you may not even end up making a purchase if the sales associate doesn't at least meet your expectations in this regard.

Yes, I understand the concept of self-improvement. It wouldn't be called that if there wasn't some personal ownership there. All I'm saying here for you sales managers is to be an active sales manager. Take a participatory role in each of your salespeople's personal development. Coach them to increase their sales ability and watch their self-assurance levels rise.

When you do this, you are on the right path to guide them to deliver the numbers.

LESSON 7: PROTECT THE CORPORATION

Always do right. This will gratify some people
and astonish the rest.
—Mark Twain

I had the pleasure of working for 3M Company for seventeen years in sales, sales training, and sales management positions. 3M is a great company because they truly understand this foundational principle: *people are an organization's greatest asset.* Not only does 3M understand this principle but it is enacted upon regularly. The investment in people on a consistent basis via training programs and the opportunity for self-learning were always available to me and my sales team.

One of those opportunities was a session on ethics in business as part of a sales manager's meeting in St. Paul. I remember we were in a large lecture hall on the 3M campus, and the session was facilitated by one of 3M's attorneys and an outside guest speaker. While the content of the presentation focused on good decision-making and appreciation for a code of conduct, both internally and externally, one segment rang true with me and still does to this day.

Protect the Corporation. This learning lesson focused on internal and external communications, with a specific emphasis on what is put in writing and shared with customers and constituents. The concept in a nutshell is to ensure you are honest; operate with the best interest of the company in mind while providing a fair and equitable communication with your customers. Should there be disagreement internally on process, direction, or territory disputes, keep your customers out of those discussions. Simply put: Don't air your dirty laundry with your customers. Don't share your internal disagreements with outside sources. Don't discuss internal affairs with the competition. Do always maintain professionalism. Do treat your colleagues with respect.

So, while I've carried this important learning with me throughout the years, I am still amazed at the number of times I've seen people vent their indiscreet opinions in writing with external sources and share that same message internally with co-workers. This scenario is even more predominant since social media has taken over as the number-one communication option for this business generation.

Mind you, I'm a big proponent of the First Amendment, the freedom of speech. I have a degree in journalism and worked for a newspaper at one point in my career. Certainly, I support whistleblowers and the laws that protect individuals who come forward to report illegal operations. Heck, if everybody just went along without speaking up at times, then that would be even worse. A little conflict when controlled is good for the organization; there is nothing wrong with a difference of opinion.

What I'm focused on here is the concept of using the right filter to express one's opinion in a professional manner that keeps the infighting in, and the outside parties removed from the disturbance. My proposal for your thoughts: Abuse of personal freedom at the expense of others is irresponsible; at the expense of the corporation, it is terminable.

I've seen a lack of discretion in communication way too much lately. Being opinionated is one thing. Sharing that opinion with external sources and hiding behind tenure is another. Too many people operate with a "sense of entitlement" that tears at the very core of a company. They operate in an unfiltered, uncensored, and uncontrolled manner, but what really bugs me most is that they have no sense of the ramifications of their actions. They've gone rogue with no understanding of the damage they are doing to the overall operation. I find this behavior *absolutely unacceptable*.

I am focused on the sales managers who are reading this lesson. Keep your internal disputes internal. Keep your customers out of the fray. Be careful what you share with external sources such as former employees, news publications, and competitors. Better still, if you can avoid talking to the competition outside of doing a little secret shopping, take that approach all the time.

Protect your sales team, and ensure they understand the principle of protecting the corporation. As a leader, you have an obligation to the company that pays you to be mindful of your internal and external presentation. Even if you disagree with direction, find the right method of expressing your opinion to the right people to let them know perhaps there is a better solution. Perhaps there is a better way. But above all, protect your colleagues and the corporation.

If you find yourself typing a scathing email with the intent of venting your frustrations, follow the Lincoln Rule. Type the email (in Lincoln's case, it was "write the letter"), get it all out, vent to your heart's desire, throw everyone possible under the bus, read it over a few times, and then file it away. *Do not address the e-mail to anyone in particular. Do not press send.* Better still, delete it all together. You'll feel good about writing and will feel even better about not sending.

Public perception of your workplace is partially your responsibility and partially the responsibility of everyone with whom you work. If you have someone on your team or if there is someone in your organization who abuses their personal freedom at the expense of others and your operation, do everything you can legally to get them removed from your company. They don't belong there in the first place. Your organization will be far better off once they're gone.

And in your case, you can be proud to implement the core premise: Protect the Corporation.

LESSON 8: IT'S ALL ABOUT HAVING AN ATTITUDE—A POSITIVE ONE

I can alter my life by altering the attitude of my mind.

If you know anything at all about golf, you know it can be a humbling game. It's hard. Let me clarify. It's hard to be good at golf. To be successful at this game, you must be able to put in the time required to deliver positive results. The only way you get better at golf is to practice and to work on your swing with the intent of consistently repeating the correct effort to deliver desired results.

There are several people I know who would say the mental aspect of golf is even harder to master than the physical aspect. While perfect practice can provide the groundwork for a solid golf swing, one mental error on the golf course, and the next thing you know you're writing down an eight on the scorecard. The dreaded snowman. Very humbling. Especially on a par 3 when you put your first two tee shots in the water, reach the green in 5, and 3-putt. Loads of fun.

Yet golf is one of those recreational opportunities that keeps me coming back for more. No, I don't like being humiliated. It's just the challenge of the game that I enjoy. And of course, all it takes is one or two good shots in a round, one or two birdies, and I'm hooked. I'll be back.

What keeps me coming back most of all, however, is my approach to playing golf. I am nowhere near what anyone would consider to be a good golfer. I broke 80 one time in my life. Yep, a 79. I kept the scorecard for years, but it went by the wayside during one of my cross-country moves. I knew all along I would never be a professional golfer, regardless of how much practice time I put in or how mentally prepared I could possibly be to play the game.

I play golf for fun. I don't take it too seriously. I never gamble or make bets while on the golf course. I don't drink alcohol on the golf course. I relax and enjoy the surroundings and laugh at my golf inequities and laugh even harder when I total my score. But it doesn't bother me. Why? Because I have the right attitude about playing golf. They don't pay me to play, so I can't take it too seriously.

What I do take seriously is how I behave on the golf course. I don't throw clubs when I hit a bad shot. I used to. I don't swear and berate the golf gods if I lose a ball in the water. I used to. I don't slump in the cart and allow my body language to dictate a negative attitude. I used to. My attitude is completely different. What's changed?

Simple answer: Maturity.

More complex answer: Positive approach to difficult challenges.

It took a while, but I had an awakening during a round of play several years ago. We approached a relatively challenging par 5, measuring 545 yards from the white tees with water running parallel nearly the entire length left of the narrow fairway and the largest natural forest known to mankind on the right of the fairway. To complicate matters more, the fairway sloped at approximately a twenty-degree angle from the forest to the middle of the safe driving area. Scattered at various intervals within that slope were fairway bunkers, sand traps, little patches of beach positioned at the precisely calculated distance from the tee box to provide full intimidation to the weekend golfer. If you hit too far right, you were in the woods. If you hit too far left, you were in the drink. If you managed to rifle a ball toward the slope, you may end up hitting your second shot with a long iron from the sand. That's one of those "Gee, I wished I practiced that shot" opportunities. So, in order to be safe from the tee box, you had to hit your drive just left of where the slope levels off and the water begins.

Pretty narrow safety chute, a challenge, but doable.

Except not so much so for my partner, who said the following as we approached the tee box: "I have trouble with this fairway."

At that precise moment, it was a revelation to me. Here's what I thought about his statement: yes, indeed, you certainly do. You will have trouble with this fairway if that's the way you are going to approach this challenge. You have already convinced yourself that you will not be successful. You placed a negative thought in your mind that will limit your actions. There is no way you can hit a good shot here.

Based on his statement and thinking, he had already convinced himself that this challenge was too much to overcome. He put himself in a defeatist position before he even tried to hit his shot. Perhaps he was just being a bit of a realist based on past performance but come on. How would you expect to improve your game and overcome this challenge with that negative stimulus firmly planted in your mind?

Sure enough, he positioned himself to aim right in order to play a minor hook, which was part of his normal swing. Too much right arm coming over the top. He took a vicious cut, promptly overswung, and hooked his ball too far to the left of center. The results were inevitable. His tee shot rifled into the water at a tremendous velocity. Once it hit the water, it didn't just drop in and down. It hit hard on a line with the water's surface and skipped and skipped and skipped, just like one of those flat rocks you throw at the beach. A few splashes, and then it disappeared into the pond. Bass bait. Turtle trouble.

I didn't laugh, but oh, I wanted to. I didn't say "oops," but oh, I wanted to. I didn't even provide any professional commentary, as competitive weekend golfers sometimes tend to do, by saying something like "That one's wet," or "You got ahold of that one; too bad it wasn't straight."

I just stood there, silent.

My partner provided all the verbal abuse required to perfectly describe the situation.

While he attempted to calm down, I returned to the cart and changed clubs. No way was I going to hit a driver on this hole. I didn't need to "muscle up." All I needed to do was hit it safe and straight. I pulled out my three-wood, the club I felt that day to have the most control. Walked to the tee box. Took two practice swings. Picked a spot just left of the slope. Cleared my thoughts. Swung nice and easy and delivered a ball left center, in the fairway, 225 yards from the tee. Not the farthest drive, certainly not the best hit, but for this situation it was perfect. That day I learned the most valuable lesson I've ever learned on a golf course: positive thoughts help you believe to achieve.

Of course, this premise is a life lesson, one to be ingrained for in our memories.

For driving through the everyday grind of sales and sales management, it is a mandatory requirement to be successful. I say this because as the leader of the sales team, the manager is always setting the pace for the team and is looked upon for how the team responds to situations and challenges. If the manager takes the positive approach to problems, the team certainly has a role model from whom to build on to take the same type of approach. The team feeds on the perceived outward actions of the leader.

The more positive the leader, the more positive the team.

If you don't believe this simple statement, ask yourself for whom you would rather work—glass half full or half empty?

Better still, how about the person who sees both half full and half empty and figures out how to fill it up?

People will work tirelessly for leaders who have vision and who believe in success.

Throughout my career, I've had the unique opportunity to work with, for, and supervise a variety of individuals who owned an array of attitudes, ranging from ultra-positive to downright devilishly negative. Some of the best of those people were at the top of the attitude chart daily. Every project and every challenge was met with the same level of positive behavior and professional approach to getting the job done. Of course, I enjoyed working with those people much more than those who didn't share the same level of positive approach. But it's not a matter of whether I liked working with them.

What matters is the attitude I maintained while leading them. By nature, I am a glass-half-empty, critical-of-others kind of guy. Not very good. Not who I really want to be. And perhaps behind closed doors, I let my frustrations vent, and my thoughts ramble down the road to negativity, but in front of them, and while coaching them, and while providing feedback, and while in strategy discussions, the concept was to always maintain the image. Stay positive. Stay focused on the goal. Keep the team motivated by setting the example that we will achieve our goal. The object was to approach every issue and every challenge with an attitude of how we can, instead of why we can't.

Have you ever been in a meeting with someone who has a clear-cut history and knowledge of why things don't get accomplished in an organization? They can religiously cite the challenges, problems, difficulties, barriers, and obstacles that prevent the organization from overachieving. They have it down to a science. Look for them in your next meeting. Listen to their words. Take copious notes. They're giving you the game plan of how things ought not to be. They are describing the history. But then listen carefully. See if they offer any solutions. Oh, they're great at detailing the problem...but not at offering options, strategies, plans, ideas, and executions for solutions. They have the negative approach to the business challenge down to a science. *Do not be a sales manager of that order!* (If you want to have some fun with them in the meeting, acknowledge their position and then ask them this question, "How do you propose we solve these issues?" Your call out should lead to a great vent.)

Sales managers, if you must detail the company challenges with the team, do it in as positive a manner as you can. Don't sugarcoat it. Just state the issues, and then follow up with statements that affirm your commitment to solving the challenges. Something like, "While I realize these are challenging issues, I believe we can move into a better position by doing these three things immediately..."

And in so doing, stay positive, with your focus on the end results. How you come across to the team is as critical an issue as how the team delivers the desired results. And regardless if you play golf or not, keep positive thoughts in your mind in all situations regardless of past performance or potential negative influences. You choose your attitude, no one does that for you. Others will perceive your attitude and make assumptions. Choose a positive attitude and let them make a correct assumption.

LESSON 9: HAVE FUN

Sometimes you need to lean on the shovel.

Epic Systems Corporation—Epic for short—based out of Verona, Wisconsin, is a privately held healthcare systems organization employing nearly ten thousand people. Hospitals that use the Epic software system account for 54 percent of patients in the United States. Epic drives MyChart, the operating system that allows you to manage your health care services with your doctor's office. Epic is a $2.9 billion company founded by CEO Judith Faulkner in 1979 and is what I would call a destination company: a company that is the epitome of what a modern, exciting, and value-driven organization provides to its employees and the marketplace.

Simply said, Epic is a place where people want to work.

Epic ranks right up there with Google, Apple, LinkedIn, and Facebook as organizations that attract people because they have a viable, profitable business model and are experts at what they do. And like those other organizations, Epic attracts people because it is a fun place to work. Placing emphasis on employee benefits, comfortable and trendy work environments, perks designed with focus on work-life balance, and a commitment to collaboration, Epic is at the forefront of a company that understands the importance of creating a community for its workers and takes good care of that community.

Epic's leadership team "gets" the definition of positive culture and what that culture means for a business. They live it, support it, own it, and promote it twenty-four seven.

What's great also about Epic is that they employ my son Christopher in the IT securities department. I am eternally grateful for Epic providing him a wonderful job and for affording me the opportunity to visit the Epic campus. All those things you hear and read about Epic being a great place to work on the grounds of a truly amazing campus are true and legitimized once you get a tour of the Epic campus.

I am still in amazement and disbelief over the work environment and campus itself, which occupies over 1,100 acres in the rolling hills just outside of Madison, Wisconsin. On the surface, there are twenty-two office buildings, two large service food centers, a training center with sixty-five training rooms, and a 5,800-seat auditorium. Five clusters of buildings with their own names and "themes" set this campus apart from others. There's the Storybook campus, Prairie Campus, Central Park Campus, Farm Campus, and Wizards Academy Campus. These are not just office buildings. In the storybook part of the campus, there is a building with an *Alice in Wonderland* theme, and one likened to Harry Potter in the Wizards Academy part of campus. All parts of the campus are decorated and furnished according to their theme. The main cafeteria and dining area is replicated to Kings Cross, modeled after the London, England, train station. There's even a castle, complete with turret, that provides an opportunity to view the campus and surrounding landscape with a several-mile view. There's an underground parking garage that is fashioned like something from *Star Trek*, which includes a deep-space-themed 11,400-seat auditorium worthy of being one of the most modern luxurious venues available for use in the Midwest. The area for downtime includes hammocks, swings, comfy chairs and sofas, and even a carousel. When I visited Epic, I wasn't sure if I was touring an amusement park or a place of employment. What I came to realize during the tour was I was experiencing a little bit of both in a unique and compatible blend that works for employees and visitors alike. Epic did a great job in creating their work environment. Anything and everything you can imagine as being part of a company's headquarters in the traditional sense is transformed into a unique experience and presented in a creative environment.

Epic is a cool place to work. It looks and feels like a fun place to work.

It offers, appeals to, and attracts the "new" employee, one who enjoys coming to work not only for the satisfaction of the job but also for the environment and established culture. Epic provides a working environment that leads me to believe they know how to have fun. While the company itself is in a highly competitive business, one that requires immense attention to detail and information security, my perception is the leadership understands there can be a balance between serious productivity and happy employees. It is easy to see how Epic employees would want to be engaged in their work. They have personal freedom, a relaxed dress code, a comfortable work environment, and exceptional perks. In exchange for these benefits, leadership expects the integrity of the business to be upheld, the work to be completed accurately and the culture to be embraced. Epic's mission statement is simply "Do good." Based on what they've created, it certainly provides a reason for employees to want to do just that and more.

Which brings me back to reality. Not every company has the resources to provide an environment like Epic. Not everyone can work for a company like Epic. Every company wants their employees to be productive, get the job done, and enjoy the work environment and company culture in exchange for an acceptable wage. Every employee wants to be appreciated, have an opportunity for advancement if desired, and wants to be treated with respect in a safe and comfortable work environment.

Having fun while at work can provide a balance between what the company is able to offer and what the employees want. Having fun at work with the intent to provide balance in the environment can come in a variety of ways.

OK, so maybe the company for which you work doesn't have a Kings Cross–themed cafeteria. Maybe you don't even have a cafeteria on campus. But that shouldn't prevent you from being creative and finding ways to provide a meal service for your employees' benefit. Oh, and that includes management as well. Food days, potlucks, cook-offs, food trucks onsite, company-sponsored on-site lunches, and picnics are all opportunities for employees to engage and share camaraderie. Food always brings people together. Great food keeps people wanting to come back together.

Company-sponsored community events are other ways to engage employees and have fun in doing so. As a sales manager, I participated in numerous company sponsored events designed to "give back" to the community. These events served a dual purpose, as they created a common bond with my fellow employees while providing me a feeling that I was doing something good for the benefit of someone else. Very powerful, very fulfilling.

I participated and was the company leader and sponsor for the American Heart Association Heart Walk. My coworkers and I packed food for the Feed My Starving Children organization for those in need. I raised money for Juvenile Diabetes Research Foundation and American Cancer Society Research via golf outings and rallies. I participated in and organized donations for the Salvation Army and tagged Christmas trees with ornament gift donations for needy children. Along with my coworkers at a national training meeting, I assembled bicycles for underprivileged children. There are numerous opportunities to donate time and effort to bring coworkers together, help someone else, and have fun at the same time.

Most fun of all those opportunities however was Paint Your Heart Out in Tampa. This is an opportunity whereby about forty of my coworkers and I were provided the necessary equipment and support to paint a house, tidy up the landscaping, and clean up the homeowner's property because they didn't have the funds to do so or were of an age that prevented them from doing so. The most fun I had in these events was using a power buffer and washer to clean the sidewalk in front of a person's house. Taking a Saturday to paint someone else's house doesn't sound like fun until you do the job. When you see the final product and then see the look of joy and expression of thankfulness on the part of the homeowner, you know your time with your coworkers was well spent.

Don't have the funds to participate in community-sponsored events? Then perhaps there are some little things that don't cost much but once implemented can assist in providing a fun work environment. Workspace decorating contests, Friday afternoon minigolf in the aisles, employee talent contests, art contests, recipe exchanges, once-a-week management-led employee recognition, and reward gatherings are all options to increase engagement and allow for a fun environment. Celebrating birthdays and work anniversaries are a given for those who don't object to publicizing these events. It doesn't have to be elaborate; it just needs to be a sincere acknowledgment with thankfulness and a sense of appreciation.

How about bringing in guest speakers from the community to present a lunch and learn about financial wellness, health well-being, or safety first at home and in the workplace? Perhaps an off-site gathering to go bowling, play minigolf, or attend a play or movie?

If you agree that a balanced blend between fun and work is important to your environment and your employees' well-being, but are having challenges figuring out what to support, I suggest getting a cross-functional team of your employees together and let them brainstorm some ideas for you for assistance. I guarantee this group will come up with options, both reasonable and outrageous, which, when agreed upon, approved, and implemented, will provide more fun in the workplace.

It shouldn't be too hard to determine how to have fun at work, but if all else fails, here's one last thing you may consider. To this day, it is the one in which I took a huge risk and enjoyed a huge personal reward. Mind you, I was the vice president of enrollment, leading a diverse group of four-hundred-plus individuals in a call center environment. The work in the call center, as you would expect, was nonstop phone activity. It was hard work for the call center agents, and there was very little downtime outside of breaks or lunch time. There was an expectation set by the owner that work came first, second, and third, and if you weren't on the phone, you were costing the company an opportunity to make money. Gradually, that management style lightened up over the course of time while I was employed at that organization, so there was more emphasis placed on creating a balanced environment. Having fun at work was half-heartedly accepted.

So, with that in mind, I took a risk. Along with several of my co-worker management types, I formed "The Chains," a karaoke singing group. We wore dark sunglasses, headbands, athletic shoes, knee-length shorts, and fluorescent T-shirts. Julia "Lil' Chain", Colleen "Off the Chain", and yours truly, as my alter ego "Rusty Chain," were the singers. Dan "The Man" handled the sound machine and video production, while Dr. Bob provided the microphones, speakers, and "security." I used popular songs and rewrote the lyrics to conform to the call center environment. We then either did a video that could be shown at a meeting or distributed via the company intranet, or we performed live. The live performances were the best.

We advertised our upcoming performance date and time via posters and emails, and when the time came, we would gather as many of the call center employees who could possibly get away from their desks at the time for a "Chains Live" performance. We had one of the managers warm up the crowd that had gathered by the pre-set-up stage. He would introduce us, and on cue, we would arrive to loud cheers and whistles walking single file from another part of the office that led to the stage area. We walked through the crowd, led by several coworkers dressed in all black, who, under Dr. Bob's direction, functioned as our security team.

No one touched "The Chains."

Once on the stage, we entertained, we showboated, we danced, we engaged, we laughed, and we had people laughing with us. Thank goodness, Lil' Chain could hold a note; she could sing. As a former athlete, Off the Chain added a level of energy and enthusiasm, which was contagious. She could get the crowd dancing along. For me, I told a few jokes, kept the performance going as rehearsed along with a few ad libs, and basically tried to keep up with my two much younger counterparts. All in all, it was fun to perform, fun to be a part of, and fun for the call center team. We let down our guard and took a risk at embarrassing ourselves, all for the good of the organization and for the opportunity to have fun.

It worked on almost all counts. I'm still not sure if the owner of the company ever really bought into the concept of "The Chains" and what we were doing to lighten things up in the call center. He never came to any of our performances, nor did he ever mention or question me about the aftereffects. I believe he didn't care.

I stored the karaoke lyrics I wrote to roughly a dozen songs and occasionally will reread them from time to time just to relive those memories. Those were great times, and the fun I had during those opportunities helped keep me going in tough times. I know it helped build camaraderie among the management team and the call center workers. They appreciated our efforts to provide a bit of entertainment as a brief break in the day.

The lesson learned is simple: work doesn't always have to be all work. There is a right time and place for fun to enter the equation as well.

And as far as Epic goes, if you get the opportunity to take a tour, do so with eyes wide open. You won't be disappointed and will most likely come away with a great sense of an organization that appreciates and knows how to engage its employees.

LESSON 10: MY FAVORITE INTERVIEW QUESTION

Think all you speak but speak not all you think.

Of all the tasks and responsibilities to which a sales manager is accountable, my opinion is none is more important than hiring the right people. In my mind, making great hiring decisions to ensure you have the best people on the team should be at the core of every sales manager's strategic plan.

In looking for a new sales associate the sales manager must consider a variety of factors to find the individual that "fits" into the organization.

Some of those factors may include:

- Past performance: A history of success depending on the difficulty of the job for which the person is being interviewed.
- The ability to communicate in an enthusiastic, clear, and meaningful manner is critical to the candidate's perceived credibility.

- Examples of being organized and a good time manager with the ability to multitask, problem-solve, and specifically to be flexible to the customer's needs make a candidate more suitable in my eyes.
- Positive attitude with a propensity for diplomatic persistency and a desire for achievement. Yes, I want to hire a results-oriented, competitive person.
- Willingness to learn and show a passion for the product or service being sold. I would never hire an individual who does not believe in the product or service.

A skilled sales manager will use situationally based questions to guide the interview and determine if the candidate meets the job description requirements. Direct questions that start with "Tell me about a time…" or "Please give me an example of…" are to the point and are designed to help an interviewer gauge the experience level of the candidate.

However, there's one question that I hope every sales manager is asking their potential new representatives. It's not situational. It doesn't ask for an example. It should be the last question asked in the prepared interview.

It's my favorite: "What will you do if you don't get this job?" It's my favorite question because it is theoretical yet foundational, and it is a test of selling skills all at the same time.

You would be surprised how many people immediately react and say they will continue to look for another position, keep searching for another job, another opportunity. They didn't take the time to think it through. They just take it at its root core. When they say this, the red flags go up.

The savvy and experienced sales professional will treat this question like an opportunity, an objection, an opening in which to uncover more information to zero in on the close. "What will you do if you don't get this job" is an opportunity question for the candidate to "sell" himself or herself to the hiring manager. Of course, the whole interview process itself is about positioning and selling oneself, but this question is a real softball for the true sales professional.

The response I am looking for from the person across the table is to diplomatically pursue me in two ways:

1) What's preventing me from hiring the candidate?
2) Here's why I should hire that candidate.

This is a sales position! I expect the person across the table to sell me on why I should hire them. If they can't uncover my objections to hiring them or expound on the benefits of why I should hire them, then guess what…why would I think they could sell my product or service? Why should I hire that person? It seems to me there is no commitment to my company. My objective is to differentiate those individuals who are just looking for a job from those who want to work for my company. (Thank goodness, Mr. Stern didn't ask me the "What will you do if you don't get this job" question.)

When asked the question, I would expect something like this as a solid answer: "I appreciate what you are saying. Making great hiring decisions is essential to your responsibility and commitment to your company. You want the best on your team. So, before you make the final decision, I'd like to reiterate my interest in this position and determine if there is something that is still in question regarding my skill set? [Pause.] If agreed, then allow me the opportunity to reinforce my credentials and abilities because I came here to earn this job, to be part of this organization, and be part of your team."

If all else is good, *sold!* Hire this person as soon as possible. And while the above answer may be a bit formal, a savvy sales manager will recognize a legitimate candidate's natural and sincere response delivered with a reasonable effort and the intent to sell the candidate's skill set to the sales manager.

Many interview questions are tests, and in order to pass that test, the potential candidate better put on the sales hat and be sharp enough to uncover what I am after: a salesperson who's not afraid to ask for the business.

LESSON 11: COMMUNICATE WINNING: SET THE PACE

*You cannot sit on the road to success, for
if you do, you will get run over.*

If you google "leadership communications," you will find results that number in the hundreds of millions. This broad terminology obviously has a major online presence based solely on the numerous articles on the subject matter.

Toastmasters defines leadership communications as being focused on the "messages from the leader that are rooted in the core values and culture of an organization and are of significant importance to key stakeholders, e.g., employees, customers, strategic partners, shareholders, and the media." *

One of my favorite examples of poor leadership communications came to me one day while listening to the sports segment on the local news back in the day while living in Chicago. Growing up in the Windy City made it easy to get engrained

* (westsidetoastmasters.com/resources Part 1: Developing the Leadership Message, Chapter 1: What is Leadership Communications)

in Chicago's professional sports teams. The NFL's Bears, the NHL's Blackhawks, the NBA's Bulls, and of course the north side's MLB's Cubs. Yes, there is a baseball team on the south side of Chicago as well. I believe they're called the White Sox, which should clearly tell you where my allegiances lie. If someone tells you they are a fan of both the Cubs and the Sox, you know that person is not from Chicago. But let's not digress to a disagreement about which baseball team owns Chicago, and all joking aside, let me provide you an example of ineffective leadership communications from the Chicago Bears Management team of the early 2000s, literally the Monsters of the Midway.

I love the Bears. Being a child of the sixties, I was around when they won the championship in '63. I lived and died with them throughout numerous ups and downs, especially when they went 1–13 in '69 and were the worst team in professional football. I watched their comebacks in the '70s and partied hard when they won their first Super Bowl after the '85 season. I nearly froze to death at the ancient Soldier Field watching Walter Payton, the greatest running back of all time, single-handedly lead his team to the playoffs. However, as many great players that the Bears employed on the field, their senior leadership was equally bad off the field.

During the sports segment I mentioned earlier, the local reporters were interviewing Bears president Ted Phillips and then–general manager Jerry Angelo about who they were interviewing to be the next Bears head coach. They had it down to three candidates, including Nick Saban, Russ Grimm, and Lovie

Smith. When asked about the goals of the organization reaching a decision to hire one of the finalists, as best as I can remember the response from the podium came across something like this: "We want to hire someone who will help us keep pace with the Packers, Vikings, Lions, the North Division of the league…" Again, I nearly froze to death. Upon hearing this catastrophe of a statement, I immediately shut off the radio. I was so aggravated; I am still amazed I was able to keep my car on the road.

Seriously? Keep pace? Why not just tell everybody right then and there that you want to be mediocre? How about this? Let's just be good enough to keep the fans interested. Why not just say we don't need to win, we just need to be good enough to stay even with our competition?

Hell no. What I expected to hear from the leaders and senior management of the Bears organization is very simple. I expected them to say they were going to hire the best coach available who would guide the team to win. I wanted them to say they were going to Set the Pace, not just keep pace!

I wanted them to say that they were going to hire the person who will lead the team to beat the Green Bay Packers twice in the same season, beat the Vikings twice in the same season, beat the Lions twice in the same season, win the North Division, win the NFC Championship, and win the Super Bowl!

I expected that the leaders of the organization would tell the media and those millions of Bears fans that the plan was simple: bring in the best coach who would help the team *win*!

They didn't. But someone in the organization was thinking along the same lines as many of us who heard those words from the Bears "management," as evidenced a few days later when the Bears hired Lovie Smith as head coach.

At Coach Smith's introductory press conference, he announced in a very calm, unemotional, serious, and genuine demeanor that his three goals as coach of the Bears were to beat the Packers, win the NFC North, and win the Super Bowl.

Faith restored. All is well with Chicago Bears football again. Media disaster avoided. I'm back on the road, being a courteous and observant driver.

Now what has this story got to do with sales management? Everything, if you consider that what you say to your team in any given situation is basically "book." They rely on you to be the clear voice of reason and the rock of all things positive. They expect you as a leader to present the plan to *win*. They may be the ones accountable for executing the plan, but you must be the one who creates and owns the plan...and it better be focused on winning.

That means winning the sales battles as a team. Winning for the betterment of the organization and for the health and well-being of the office staff. Winning as in "this is our culture"— we only hire winners here. Winning is at the very core of what we do here to have fun and be excited about coming to work.

Trying hard can be fun. Trying hard and winning is ultimately satisfying.

Sales managers, when you are in front of your team always, always, always talk about winning as a team. While you establish a variety of goals, both personally and professionally, you ensure that your team knows you are serious about winning. That you are serious about delivering the goods for the company, and that together, there is no greater sense of accomplishment than establishing a major goal and winning by achieving that goal.

I made an earlier comment about winning as a culture in an organization. The best companies have that premise ingrained in their playbook—sometimes referred to as an employee handbook, if they even have one—but mostly it's just a way of being, thinking, acting, and living. When you believe in winning, the winning becomes much easier.

My Bears have yet to repeat as Super Bowl Champions, but hope remains. The Cubs broke a 108-year drought by winning the World Series in 2016. The Blackhawks won three Stanley Cups during the past decade. The Sox last won in 2005, and the Bulls glory days are long gone from their six championships.

So, I'll leave you with this fact regarding a sports franchise that ingrains winning into their culture. Love them or hate them...the New York Yankees have won twenty-seven World Series titles, more than twice as many as their nearest runner-up (name unmentioned; look it up).

My younger son, Corey, worked for the Yankees organization for a while, and from day one as an employee, he learned "the Yankee Way," a culture established around professionalism with winning at its core. As a sales manager, much can be learned from creating your own document that details "Our Business Way" or "Our Winning Way," so if anything, at least the sales team is on board and focused on winning.

Winning is a way of being. Winning ethically is a statement of culture. Winning is a result of hard work, focus, dedication, commitment, intensity, execution, and desire. Winning as a team is the ultimate reward for a sales manager. Take the time to define what winning looks like for you, your team, and your organization. Then, Set the Pace to win every day.

LESSON 12: ALWAYS BE RECRUITING: BUILD YOUR TEAM, IMPACT YOUR TURNOVER

There are people who make things happen, people who wait for things to happen, and people who don't know anything happened.

It never fails to happen, and it happens routinely. Unfortunately, it happens all too often at the expense of the sales manager and the organization. While the diligent sales manager is focused on driving results, a situation occurs that does more damage to the sales manager's operation than she cares to admit. A top sales representative on the manager's team submits his two-week notice. He explains he really enjoys working with the organization, yet just received an offer he couldn't pass up. As a matter of fact, he's been talking to his new company for some time now. They contacted him through a "talent acquisition agency" (fancy words for what I would commonly refer to as a headhunter) and the opportunity is something that just seems right for him to pursue. He thanks the manager for her professionalism and dedication and, above all, her commitment to him achieving results and for committing to his personal development. He wishes her well in her future endeavors. He knows not to burn any bridges; after all, his new dream job just may be more of a nightmare than a pleasant experience, so he leaves on a good note with the door open for a return and reference if necessary.

From the sales manager's perspective, she now wonders what went wrong. Why would the rep leave? Hadn't she spent time with him, showed him the ropes? Provided a learning environment? Contributed to his development? Pushed him and prodded him when he needed a bit of direction to achieve the numbers and recognized him for his accomplishments? Wasn't she the one who explained the numbers to him and spent time on sales calls with him and his customers? Heck, she even worked with him in taking a lead role in contributing to the new hires' learning experience by participating in training programs and as a mentor for one newbie who shows a great amount of potential. So, if she followed her plan with this rep, what happened? Why is he leaving? What has she done wrong as a sales manager?

Obviously, there are several answers to her questions and many variables that could influence the decision to leave the organization for perceived greener pastures. Perhaps the offer which the rep received really is his dream job with unlimited opportunity for advancement. Maybe the sales manager did everything she possibly could do to ensure her investment in her sales representative would pay dividends for the organization. Yet maybe there is something missing.

Maybe during her diligence in creating a career path for this rep she spent too much time focused on him as an individual contributor to the bottom line, and not enough time focused on him as a person as he exemplifies an important issue in any organization: having the right people on the team. While she thought she was spending time making an investment in his development, perhaps the rep's perception was that her effort was more focused on driving him to produce results based on the manager's reasons and not his. What I am trying to say here is that while the sales manager may never really know the individual rep's motivation for leaving an organization, the manager must be aware of the importance of treating people as people first, and assets second.

It is pretty much accepted that people leave an organization based on their relationship with their direct manager. If they like their manager, odds are they stay with the company, provided the compensation, benefits, working environment, and the other variables that comprise an opportunity are equitable in the eyes of the beholder. If they don't like their manager, odds are they leave the organization, try to move to another part of the organization, or in some cases, stick it out to see if they can outlast the manager in hopes of having her replaced with someone who may be of better interest to their concerns.

They may say they leave for perceived greener pastures— more opportunity for advancement, better salary, promotional career paths, leadership and responsibility, or a plethora of other reasons—but the basic reason usually revolves around the employee's relationship with their direct supervisor. The true sales manager is one who understands the concept of driving for a balance between chasing the numbers and developing the people. If the sales manager places too much emphasis on obtaining the numbers, the team never really feels appreciated. Too much emphasis on the people side of the business, and the team may take advantage of the situation and the manager.

In fact, the manager who only focuses her efforts on the results portrays herself as not really caring about those who produce the results. The savvy sales manager knows the business relies upon the people who generate the numbers, and she knows her existence depends upon her relationship with those result producers. If she is focused on results through people, she stands a much better chance of succeeding than if she is limited to an approach based on just the numbers.

This is a very simple premise, and I am sure many of you reading this section are thinking just that. Heck, it is foundational and perhaps a principle one learns in the first week of manager prep school. Yet it is amazing to me how many people I have come across who don't follow this basic principle in leading their teams. Some sales managers are so driven by obtaining the results that they are apt to steamroll over the very core of the sales team and are not even aware of their own shortcomings. While focusing on the numbers, they lost sight of the need to ensure their approach to the business at hand revolves around their interaction and relationship with their team. The most successful sales managers I know are those who recognize their success is measured by their commitment to the development of their individual team members. They are the ones who fully grasp the concept of results through people by creating an environment that establishes mutual respect, loyalty, and team determination. They are the ones who set the example by doing little things such as saying good morning to each of their teammates every morning, not just on days when they feel great and wish to share their morning cheer. Little things like this simple action open doors for respect and bonding. Most important, these people-oriented gestures must be genuine. The worst thing I witnessed during my thirty-plus years in sales management is the manager who is just going through the motions when it comes to the people side of the business. It comes across as so unrealistic and disingenuous that the attempt to be a people person does more damage to the relationship than good. Being genuine and acting from the heart goes a lot longer way than having a canned approach to the sales manager's role. One simply cannot just read a text and apply the concepts. A smart sales manager knows she must be believable and genuine to establish credibility.

Savvy sales managers, true leaders if you will, understand the opportunity exists at any given moment of the working day to build a personal bond with their teammates. They recognize those opportunities and consistently respect their teammates as people. They are the ones who realize accountability for the team's results is in their court and reward and recognize in public for a job well done. They take ownership of the team's results in both good times and in times when the results are less than desired. The truly effective sales manager is one who understands and recognizes the need to balance pursuit of numerical achievement and people praise.

What does this spiel have to do with our sales manager trying to figure out her recent turnover? Let's face the fact that no matter how skilled you are as a sales manager you will have turnover.

People do things for their reasons and their reasons alone, and certainly over the course of time, every sales manager realizes she will lose some great salespeople to other organizations. It's not so bad to lose those people to an internal transfer, and in fact if the opportunity is right for the individual and the organization, the sales manager-leader knows this practice can prove beneficial for a variety of reasons. While the individual moving to an opportunity in another part of the organization gets a chance to contribute in different ways and perhaps gets a promotion out of the situation, the sales manager now has several things on which to hang her hat.

First, she should be happy that she didn't stand in the way of the individual who was looking for a change or more responsibility and greater opportunity. The sales manager is perceived as a developer of people ready to assume additional responsibilities as opposed to a "blocker" standing in the way of another's opportunities. She has now contributed to the organization in a way many would say is equally as important to her making the numbers contribution. She developed an individual and prepared that person for other managers in the organization. Ultimately the sales manager is perceived as a contributor to the organization's overall goals, rather than as a person only focused on self-centered achievement.

The sales manager now also has a "seed," if you will, in another department. This seed can be a valuable asset not only to the organization but even more so to the sales manager from which the seed originated. The recently transplanted person remains loyal to the sales manager who assisted in her development and supported her opportunity and career path as a contributor to the organization. This perception bodes well for both seed and sales manager: the seed speaks highly of the sales manager's support in career path planning and development, and the sales manager has a plant in another department. Over the course of years, I learned that the best way to get something done by members of another department with which you must work is to have your own people placed successfully in those departments. It just doesn't get any better than having a person in which you spent time and energy into developing answer the phone or respond electronically when you have a request that needs fulfillment. Some of you may be thinking leverage. I prefer to say this is merely a business method that takes a partnership approach to achievement and sure beats asking cold for something to get done.

Yes, sales managers, now ask yourself the question: Have you ever stood in someone's career path and blocked their transition simply because you didn't want to lose that person's productivity from your team? Have you taken the short-sighted approach to sales management and said to yourself that this person cannot be replaced, so I must keep her in my department?

Be honest. Because if you have blocked someone for your own personal interests, you have successfully accomplished what used to be standard operating procedure in organizations that promoted a "me-first" business platform. That kind of thinking just doesn't work anymore, and I will tell you why.

The concept of getting things done or driving results through people is specifically focused on building relationships first, and in seeking to assist others in achieving their career aspirations. When you help someone get what they want, you ultimately end up getting what you want twofold. I sincerely believe in this foundational principle.

Some of you, and I hope that is a very few of you, may be thinking that while sales manager Ted is assisting his team in developing their skill set to contribute to other parts of the organization, he is losing sight of the intent and purpose of the sales department. On the contrary, it should be the intent and purpose of every sales manager to contribute to the organization by developing people to achieve and grow because those people will ultimately have the same responsibility in the future, and if they didn't learn this basic principle from experience, then the organization stands a good chance of failing in this most important aspect of management. So, while it is important to deliver results, the approach of delivering results via loyal, engaged, career-focused employees is a much better approach to business than the blocker syndrome previously described.

Sales Manager Ted wants me to develop my people, so they will be loyal, focused, engaged, and produce results, but at the same time, he wants me to get them ready to take on additional assignments in other departments. Why can't they just be great salespeople and be the best at what they do in the first place, which is sell, sell, sell?

Indeed, the calling of a professional salesperson is truly an admirable one. Those that take the role seriously are relationship oriented, client focused, results determined and willing to go the long haul for the benefits. It is those that understand the concept of "people first," whom the savvy sales manager will be able to invest time in, get results from, and be able to prepare for greater responsibilities. There is nothing wrong with great salespeople who want to stay great salespeople. Every sales manager wants and needs those individuals on the team. All I am saying here is that it is up to the sales manager to understand the team's components and identify the ones who can become great managers or leaders in other parts of the organization. And once identified, it is up to the sales manager to assist the individual in creating a plan to get them to where they want to be...at the request of the organization rather than at its expense.

In so doing, it is then the sales manager's responsibility to ensure an appropriate replacement for the team member who moved on to other options.

LESSON 13: ACT ON YOUR COMMITMENT TO RECRUIT

You won't even get started if you wait for all the conditions to be just right.

In continuing this lesson, here are a few action items and thoughts in support of the importance of recruiting for the team, and the sales manager's responsibility to deliver in this important aspect of consistent performance.

Action item 1: Have a bullpen. The savvy sales manager knows she will lose people for their reasons, and she will also lose people for the organization's reasons; heck, she may even lose people without any reason, but the real focus needs to be on the importance of always improving the team, never to remain status quo, always to add and get better.

A sales manager who recruits only when she has an available position is doing a disservice to herself, her team, and her organization. She is taking a reactionary approach rather than a proactive approach to ensuring her team remains solid and producing at the expected levels. The proactive sales manager uses network-ing opportunities to build a bullpen of resumes, contacts, and potential candidates with the intent of being prepared for those times when, for whatever reason, a sales rep leaves the team. It sounds simple, yet you know as well as I do that this proactive approach requires some work outside of the daily norm. If you have some limitations regarding being able to build your poten-tial bench, just remember the basic principle of what made you successful as a sales rep; always be prospecting. To build your client base and increase company revenue along with personal income, you knew the importance of prospecting for new busi-ness or replacement business. It is the same premise here: keep recruiting to gain new valuable members for the team, and to replace those who leave.

Action item 2: Work with your human resources team. For those of you who have an HR department that is tasked with recruiting people into your organization, stop hiding behind their accountability. When they are not supplying the number of people you need or the right kinds of people, finger-pointing is not the answer. I encourage you to work with your HR team to attract the right people to the organization and partner to deliver appropriate results. Yet I also encourage you to take your own ac-countability for the type of people you want in your organization and specifically on your sales team. You will be in a much better position when you own the process and bring your people on board. You control your destiny when it comes to hiring.

Action item 3: Recruiting the right people for your organization starts with you. You set the example for the organization when you take the time to provide viable candidates to add value to the team. You also show other managers in the organization that you are willing to take ownership for the quality of the individuals on your team and in the organization. That is a foundation of leadership, the ability to see a bigger picture for the good of the overall organization. I firmly believe that to be truly accountable for your results, you should own the process for bringing people on board in the part of the organization in which you lead. It seems simple, yet how often do we really execute on that philosophy?

I see it too often in organizations whereby managers claim to make all the hiring decisions yet are only hiring from the small pool of candidates provided by other resources like staffing firms or their internal recruiters. For those people I would ask a few questions. When was the last time you recruited someone to join your organization? You may have hired many, but did you hire your own? Did you use social networking to meet new people who may possibly provide you with quality candidates for your team or organization? How about the times you are out to dinner or at the airport or at the shopping mall—are you looking for opportunities to engage people in conversation regarding your organization? (Heck, you may even find a customer or two that way.) Recruiting candidates to work where you work should not be viewed as a task but as an obligation. If you truly are engaged in your operation, then recruiting people to work with you should be second nature simply because you care about the success of the place at which you work.

Action item 4: How engaged are you with a networking group that supports your industry and keeps you in touch with other professionals at your level? The opportunity to mix and mingle with peers provides a much-needed break away from the office to socialize on common ground. Yet don't just attend for the breakfast or lunch that your company gets for paying their monthly dues to the networking event. Use this opportunity to represent your organization and its principles. Use this opportunity to interact and discuss challenges with your peers. Most likely you will find a time where in conversation with a peer, the name of a potential candidate to add to your team, will be mentioned. Think about how you got your job. Did you go online, apply, and send a résumé like countless others who may engage in this practice? Or did you earn the right to get a referral from a well-connected counterpart to help you gain access to a key decision maker at an organization? It's sales at its basic element. Build up your network to earn and gain referrals of individuals that can be trusted, come with a recommendation, and a good portion of the recruiting job is taken care of for you. Don't you agree this is a much better approach than having to sift through countless stone-cold résumés? Aren't you more likely to find a much more qualified person for your sales team based on a tried and true referral? Getting engaged with your peers at networking events is a great way to keep filling the recruitment pipeline.

Action item 5: How about former employers and former colleagues? This question assumes you left your prior positions on good terms and was well respected by individuals with whom you worked. Now, I'm not suggesting you go back to your most recent employer and start calling all your former salespeople to come and join your new organization. Poaching is not an acceptable practice in my eyes. What I am suggesting is that you let people know of opportunities via social networking. In recent months, I've been contacted by several former coworkers who determined to move on from their employer due to market conditions, management changes, spouse relocation, and business consolidation. If you stay in touch with your network, people will reach out when the time requires them to act. Guess what? This is also a perfect opportunity to receive referrals of contacts who may be well suited to join your organization.

In summary, a sales manager knows that the commitment required to build a strong sales team starts with the effort placed in recruiting to a higher standard. Even if you have a well-tenured, highly productive team currently, there will be opportunities to add to the team due to personnel attrition or company growth. I encourage you to keep this principle at the forefront of common activities. Always be recruiting. Always be recruiting. Always be recruiting.

LESSON 14: LEAVE YOUR EGO AT THE DOOR

Son, your ego is writing checks your body can't cash.
—Commanding Officer Stinger in the movie *Top Gun*

As you would expect, I worked for a variety of managers over my forty-plus years in sales and sales management. Some of those managers turned out to be excellent leaders from whom I learned about sales and sales management and, most importantly, learned about how to treat people with respect and dignity. Several of those leaders were a pleasure to work with and certainly made me feel part of their team. They led by example and genuinely cared about their coworkers. They valued my opinion. They spent quality time with me and my team managers. They supported innovation and were open to new ideas. They promoted a productive, professional, and inclusive work environment. They were fun to work with and for and certainly made it easier to "want" to do a great job for them. They made it easy to be loyal. They were more about "we" than they were about "I" and, in so doing, provided the perfect work environment. They were trusted.

In making a list of the qualities of an effective leader in general terms I would include these descriptions, among others:

- Great vision for the company, has a long-term approach for organizational growth
- Excellent communications skills
- Genuine and empathetic to all
- Honest, ethical, and owner of integrity
- Leads by example regarding work ethic
- Knowledgeable about the overall business and the industry
- Process improvement champion
- Customer centric
- Genuinely cares about people
- Open to having fun
- Wants to win
- Results oriented, people focused, with a great understanding of the balance between these two qualities
- Accountable to self and holds others to the same standard

I'm sure we could continue this list with additional items based on your own experience with people you believe to be great leaders. As I mentioned in a previous lesson learned, I hope you work with a person who exemplifies great leadership and encourages you on a regular basis to be your best, do your best, and live your best.

However, what really hit home with me with the leaders I had the privilege to work with, was the things they didn't do that made them so effective. Remember, I'm a half-empty-glass kind of guy and have that tendency to associate and lean toward understanding the downside just a bit better. It helped me learn that "what not to do is just as important as what to do," and knowing the difference in making decisions, especially in how those decisions affect people, is critical to effective management.

As an example, a situation with one of the supposed leaders that I worked with for a short time (name withheld) taught me a valuable lesson regarding the importance of the performance appraisal process, the seriousness of legitimate and timely feedback, and most importantly, how not to blindly insert unwarranted authority.

Due to a restructuring of the company that I was working for at the time, there was a shuffling of managers to consolidate territories. My prior manager moved to a home office position for another division so my team of nine representatives and I would now report to the new regional director. This new regional director had been with the company for many years but worked in a different division and thus, while perhaps earning the right for promotion based on tenure, had no real understanding of the people or process that occurred in my operation. He had experience and reputation, and if he had taken the time to learn about my operation, he may have developed into a good manager-leader...and kept his job for a while. But he didn't. And from his actions I learned a valuable lesson.

It was performance appraisal time, and I completed the process for my nine representatives. I take this process seriously, and if done properly, it is not a surprise when delivered to those involved. There is feedback and discussion throughout the appraisal cycle, so the end results are anticipated, and the deliverable is much easier to discuss with the person being appraised. I had my work documented. It was fact based. I did observations throughout the cycle. I worked with each representative and provided feedback throughout the cycle. The appraisals I wrote were genuine, legitimate, reasonable, and honest.

Our process at the time was to have the regional director sign off on the appraisals prior to delivering to the representative. So, being that I had a new regional director, I went to the home office human resources leader and asked if I should send my appraisals to my former manager for review or to my new manager for review. I expected the answer to my query to be to send them to my former manager. But this was not to be. I was instructed to send them to my new RD; based on his experience, the sign-off would be a mere formality anyway. Wrong!

I sent my appraisals to my new RD (yes, hard copy; these were the early days before any electronic appraisal system was in place. The process was antiquated, but it's what we had to work with and was very tedious compared to the systems available today.). Anyway, I sent my appraisals and anticipated the formal sign off and return, whereby I could then meet with each of my representatives and deliver their appraisal feedback.

Much to my chagrin, the appraisals were returned to me in a few days via inter office mail. No phone call, no personal visit, no communication, no heads-up…just the appraisals, all nine of them marked in red pen—yes, red pen! My new RD decided he didn't like what I had written and wrote all over the documents with his own form of "feedback." Mind you, these were the original documents. Turns out my new RD disagreed with my assessment of my team and the ratings I provided. He was on the job less than a month but had a preconceived opinion about my operation. The only area in which he considered regarding the appraisals was the sales numbers—that's it, just the numbers. So, if a rep didn't hit their numbers, there was no way they could be a solid ambassador of the company. No way could they gain customer respect and satisfaction. No way they could conduct their business on a professional level day in and day out. No way they could get a reasonable performance appraisal. No way they would be allowed to exist in the organization, and especially, no way in the new RD's territory. Big red letters: No WAY. He wanted all the appraisals lowered by a grade to "below expectations" with the exception of the assistant manager; he wanted her appraisal lowered two grades to "underperforming," the lowest of the five available performance grades.

I blew a gasket!

To this day, I remember my reaction: Who the heck does he think he is? He comes on board, knows nothing of the operation, the people, their effort, the situations, and especially of my assessment of their ability to do the job. He has no clue about their relationships with their customers. He is simply trying to send a message: it's about him and no one else.

What really irritated me about the whole situation was the fact that my office was one of the most successful in the organization, meaning in the country as we operated in twenty-six states. We weren't resting on our laurels. We were better than most of the other offices and certainly delivered a huge amount of revenue to the company.

He just couldn't get over his own ego. He was in charge and had to let people know he was in charge.

Well, he certainly went about it the wrong way. He made a huge managerial and leadership error; he had yet to earn the right to insert himself into the appraisal process. He had yet to build trust and respect and understand the business before making a huge decision. His ego wouldn't let him learn to be a good manager and leader. What a dumb——.

And of course, me being who I am, and letting my emotions get the better of me, I promptly went over his head. Right back to the human resources person who "guided" me in the direction in the first place. At that time in my life, I wasn't afraid of career suicide and pushing back on my "boss" by using another resource. In hindsight, I should have approached him in a professional manner to talk it out. Perhaps he would have rescinded his direction, allowed me to manage my team, and we both could have formed a better relationship at that point.

Could have, should have, would have…a gambler's losing proposition.

I'll keep the HR conversation results short. I ended up winning. My former manager was brought into the conversation; she overruled my new manager. I was to deliver the appraisals as I had written. I also received my own appraisal written by my former manager. She provided me with an above-average rating based on my skill set in developing my team, professionally representing the company, and for being a hardworking, responsible sales manager.

My new manager was not pleased but had to live with the decision, and I had to somehow figure out how to win him over. I needed my job! As it turned out, I didn't have to worry about him for too long. While I was focused only on my situation and on my team, my new manager had taken the same performance appraisal approach with others in the region. Unbeknownst to me, others had pushed back to him directly, and those discussions ended up in human resources as well. Thirty days later, my new RD was no longer my new RD. He was not the type of manager-leader the higher ups in the company thought they were getting when he was promoted. He was just the opposite. In fact, he was offered the opportunity to return to a representative position, out of management completely, and ultimately accepted that role to stay out his damaged career. I don't blame the higher-ups for not doing their homework on their poor promotion choice. I don't blame them for not letting him go. I commend them for taking prompt action and doing the best damage control possible. It all worked out. I kept my job and learned about the importance of earning the right to engage in the appraisal process. Outside of title and rank, knowledge and relationship take precedent; no ego allowed.

Here's one more example. It is not so much a specific incident as a general observation of someone whose misaligned ego prevents this person from being a respected leader.

I believe you will find it easy to relate to this individual because you have worked with him previously or perhaps are working with him now. See if several or any of the following descriptions apply to someone you know, worked with, worked for, currently work with…or can't wait to get away from working with in the immediate future.

He is easily recognizable. His words and subsequent actions leave nothing to the imagination other than complete astonishment and personalized thoughts of "How did he ever get the position that he holds in this company"?

He is easy to spot in meetings because he's the one who always comes in late with the expectation that since the world revolves around him, that all present will stop what they're doing and acknowledge his presence and greatness.

He starts every meeting with "I" or "I want" or "I need" and sometimes even before saying good morning or good afternoon.

He is the loudest voice in the room, and the one who seldom has anything new to offer but talks ad nauseum simply because he likes the sound of his own voice.

He was, in his eyes, the top salesperson who offers his advice by starting sentences with "When I was in your shoes" or "Let me tell you how it should be done."

He interrupts conversations, talks down to those in lesser positions, and disrespects coworkers' discussions simply because he thinks he can.

He needs to be the center of attention, but only if there isn't any accountability that goes along with being the center of attention.

He is excessively self-centered, absorbed in his own being, conceited, with little to no time for anyone that doesn't meet his lofty expectations.

He is pompous and arrogant, ruthless and cunning, vengeful and vindictive, because he is all about himself and not willing to accept others for what they are, or for what they bring to the table.

He alienates others due to his meaningless and flamboyant approach to problem-solving.

He belittles when he should build up.

He places his needs, his wants, his desires, his goals, his objectives, his focus above all else and all others regardless of the damage his intents may do to the team.

He was given his job. He didn't earn it. He doesn't know how to make a good decision if it was told directly to him and all he had to do was say yes. He doesn't want the responsibility of being wrong or in making a mistake. His ego prevents that humanistic approach from happening.

He must have recognition, reward, credit for his team's effort when they win, and he finger-points, provides excuses, and deflects ownership when they fall short of expectations.

He is a do-nothing, an empty suit.

He glorifies in the word "boss" and lets others know him as such.

He is not a manager.

Nor is he a leader, confidant, sounding board, empathizer, visionary, or role model.

The only back he protects and covers for is his own.

The only golden rule he lives by centers on "Doing unto others before they do unto you."

He is outdated, short sighted, outbrained, and underachieved regularly, but in his own mind, he is far more advanced intellectually than any of his peers.

His is the only opinion that counts. Unless required, he does not choose a side in discussion. His silence is followed by his "I told you so" only after the outcome is determined.

His advice is free for the taking, and he gives it whether wanted or not.

He is not to be trusted. Period. End of sentence. Mic drop.

Ego is something we all have. Those who learn to control their ego understand the importance of checking it at the door when leading a sales team, or any team, for that matter. Because the results of the team are what really matter. It's not about the individual accomplishments or the personalized recognition that goes along with winning. It's about being part of something together.

Great sales managers know they are only as good as their weakest link. They also know that it is their responsibility to coach up that weak link for the benefit of the team and positive results. Allowing their ego to get in the way and making the quest about them and their own best interests is a perfect way to destroy the good of the team.

Ego, when unchecked, leads to disaster. Kind of like ultimate power leads to ultimate corruption. If any of the above thoughts resonated with you, take pride in knowing that your acknowledgment is a lesson learned.

No one in management really wants to be described in a negative manner as I did so above. Yet those who place their ego at the forefront of their management style run the risk of doing just that. Be better than that. Swallow some humble pie. Have an ounce of humility. Start your day in a positive manner by being thankful for your team and let them know you appreciate their efforts. Realize that you don't know everything and learn to learn from those around you. Carry yourself with a level of humility that others will openly see when you treat them as you would be treated. Leave your ego out of the relationship equation. Focus on guiding, assisting, helping, and leading others based on their needs, and you will experience the managerial success you desire.

LESSON 15: MAP OUT, MEASURE, AND MONITOR YOUR SALES PROCESS

Minds are like parachutes: they only function when open.

Everyone wants great results. The CEO wants more profitable revenue for the shareholders. The shareholders want an improved return on their investment. All employees want better benefits and salary increases, which are founded in continued and sustainable profit improvement. Customers want reduced prices and high-quality products that meet their needs, solve their problems, satisfy their desires. The cycle goes on and on, and the sales manager is at the hub of this wheel. Results, revenue growth that delivers sustainable bottom-line profit, rest squarely on the shoulders of the sales manager and team. It is not the type of position that is suited for those shy of pressure and scrutiny.

"Spotlight Exemplified" should be the title on every sales manager's nameplate, office door, and business card.

During that pressure and scrutiny, the sales manager is faced with a variety of daily challenges, ranging from recruiting, hiring, and training the sales team to delivering sales forecasts and budget expectations and growing revenue. In addition, there is an important exercise that demands attention at regular intervals. That exercise consists of doing a deep dive into the sales process. Taking the time to map out the sales process provides valuable information regarding current customer interaction, support, fulfillment, and opportunity. Most importantly, it allows the sales manager to discover key disconnects that hinder the sales process. Implementing action items to repair these disconnects not only improves the process but perhaps provides improved foundation for increased sales.

Process improvement stems from the manufacturing industry trying to achieve improved efficiencies and is founded in the theories of Six Sigma techniques and tools introduced by engineer Bill Smith at Motorola in the 1980s. The continuous improvement process stems from W. Edwards Deming's Total Quality Management efforts. Maybe it's the desire to win the Malcolm Baldridge National Quality Award that drives organizations to look for ways to implement high quality processes aimed at delivering improved management systems and ultimately deliver incremental results. Chicken and egg, as far as I'm concerned. All efforts in the quest for process improvement stem from the desire to deliver products and services at a reduced cost-efficient production and achieve the ultimate customer response—a purchase, followed by a repeat purchase. Make the item; deliver the product. Do it cost effectively and manufacture it efficiently.

Make a sale. Use the product. Repeat the sale. Grow the business and increase customer satisfaction. This is the ultimate process.

While manufacturing companies take the lead in paying close attention to their production process, far too many service organizations shy away from understanding their sales process and the effects, both positive and negative, it has on their customers. If you doubt what I am writing here, perhaps your own organization maps out the process at regular intervals, so congratulations on that aspect. I commend your team for making an investment of time to learn, understand, and hopefully implement improvement for your employees and customers. However, if you are now asking yourself, "Gee, I wonder when we last mapped out our process, and if we did, where is it viewable in writing?" then either you are unaware of the process or don't know if it exists in detail, or I have to place your organization in the situation as so many others: haven't done it, not important, consumes too much time, no leader said we should do it…every excuse in the book.

The fact of the matter is, mapping out the sales process takes an organizational commitment and an executable strategy. It requires leadership, diligence, and communication. Numerous stakeholders need to be involved in the process to provide input on the sales process from their point of view. A major mistake organizations make when they attempt to map out their sales process is in limiting the mapping input to the sales organization only, thereby providing a narrow focus and yielding what "*we think*" is the process. Input for mapping out the process needs to come from any and every part of the organization that so much as remotely touches a customer, from advertising and marketing to accounting and billing to customer service and delivery, and all points before, in between, and after. While it is easy to want to only include those who have first contact with customers, the process should be viewed as an organization's selling process, a bigger picture, a broader landscape that entails all operational aspects. Why? Because when information and input is gathered from all department's eyes open, light bulbs go off, understanding occurs, the aha moment of "Oh, I didn't know you guys did it that way" happens, and behold! Once again, shareholders in the organization actually feel like their input matters. They take ownership. If good things come out of the process mapping, they become reengaged, reinvigorated, renewed, reenergized and revitalized in the organization's ultimate effort: to please its customers and increase repeat profitable business.

Sales managers, I encourage you to take the lead in this process. Gather your peers, sell them on the benefits of mapping out the process from an employee engagement standpoint, knowing full well that the finished product will provide valuable information to help you identify areas of improvement and gain support from other departments to increase your sales! If you are not comfortable in leading the exercise yourself, then partner with someone who is familiar with this undertaking. Perhaps there is someone in your HR department who can assist. If not, there are numerous external options in the form of consultants, Six Sigma–trained facilitators, who, for a reasonable fee will provide a neutral third-party approach to the effort. In fact, hiring an external resource may be the best choice, since they will be responsible for setting up the input sessions, mapping out the process, and delivering the results to your organization—and saving you time.

Along with saving you time, an external resource will provide a valuable perspective by asking questions your organization may not consider or may consider as assumed in the sales process. They will bring a fresh approach to the overall process and perhaps deliver the most important perspective of all: your customer's. If mapping out your organization's selling and buying process does not include your customer's perspective, then you have wasted valuable time and performed an exercise for the sake of performing an exercise. Some may consider the selling process and the buying process two separate undertakings, and I can certainly see legitimate reasons in that brand of thinking. Yet from my perspective, if your organization fully understands how products or services move from your company into the hands of your customers then the transaction is just that: one seamless process, as it should be.

Of course, if you really want to gauge the seamlessness of your sales process, it is always best served to take a long hard look at your competition. Another major mistake I see in organizations' efforts to understand their sales processes is to simply draw a circle around their operation and reflect solely on their approach to their customers. A much better way to gain a full understanding of what's going on in the marketplace is to become a customer of your competition. If you are engaged in a mapping-out process and the facilitator asks you a question regarding how your competition does things and your answer is "I don't know," then not only have you missed the boat on benchmarking your process to the competition's, but you have also just let everyone else in the room know you are not engrained and engaged at the level you should be in your important position. The practice of secret shopping the competition has been going on for years and continues to be one of the best, if not the best method, of gaining valuable information on how things are done at the place to where you are losing market share. I suggest an immediate reconnaissance mission to your top three competitors if you haven't done so recently. I'm not saying you do this yourself, although it does make for an interesting experience if you do take on at least one opportunity to gauge your competition's efforts. Hire someone; send your spouse, significant other, partner. Get on the phone and online and become a lead for your competition. Much is to be learned from how your information is processed and reacted to, along with how your competition treats their prospective buyers from a requirement and service standpoint.

This lesson learned is not about how to map out the process. It is more about the importance of undertaking the exercise and hopefully I have provided you with some foundation in that regard. In answering the question why, here's a brief summary as to mapping out, measuring, and monitoring the sales-process-mapping effort.

Map out the process. Whether you do it by yourself, with your team, or with an external facilitator, take the time to map out your sales and buying process to gain a full understanding of how a product or service moves through your organization into the hands of your customer. Look for disconnects, those instances where breakdowns occur in communications between internal departments or moments where providing excellent customer service is short of expectations. Those areas impact performance and ultimately impact sales. Those areas, when appropriately addressed, offer opportunities for improvement that can positively impact sales. Also critical is to look for areas where your organization excels. Replicate, duplicate, copy, and expound on those areas as often as possible. Commend those who are leading those exceptional best practices and make that a standard mantra for your team and for your organization.

Measure the effectiveness of the process. Once mapped out, the question becomes "What do we do with the map?" Do we congratulate all who provided input and then go on our merry way and back to the routine daily grind? Or do we take the information, refer to it religiously and make it a standard operating procedure, while tracking the organization's performance to the process on a regular basis? Too often, exercises of this nature become just that: an exercise with no real follow-up. I encourage you as the leader in your company to make the process visible to your teammates. Show legitimate data tracking options that prove the value of fully knowing, understanding, and implementing consistency in process delivery. Make it a way of life in your company. Stick to the process. Provide comparisons to prior deliverables. By that, I mean: Have your results improved since you mapped and reviewed your selling process? Are other departments living up to expectations to help improve sales? Are you doing regular reporting of process efforts designed to keep others informed of your results and keeping the message of adherence at the forefront? Sticking to the process is critical. Telling others is paramount. Gaining commitment is ultimate.

Monitor the process for improved results or needed changes. When the difficult work of mapping out the process is completed, regular check-ins need to occur with the mapping team. These check-ins provide an opportunity for reporting on results, open communication between departments and stakeholders, and feedback in the form of new information, new ideas and strategies that must be implemented if there are challenges with the overall process improvement effort. If sales are not increasing and the process is flawless, then focus needs to be directed elsewhere. Remember that part about pressure and scrutiny? If the process is in place, perhaps those executing the process need to be changed. But let's not digress. This effort is concentrating on ensuring the customer has every seamless opportunity to buy something from your company. Monitoring the process and staying aware of customer complaints and process breakdowns provides a great opportunity to engage and correct direction. Instead of constantly putting out fires, a process-improvement-focused sales manager is making efforts to stay ahead of the problems that potentially can occur in the routine course of business transactions. Regular check-ins with a directed focus on this effort will yield positive results.

LESSON 16: GREAT TEAMS HAVE A NO-FINISH-LINE-TO-THIS-JOB MENTALITY

"I didn't come to be told I'm burning the candle
at both ends," said a patient to his doctor.
"I came for more wax."

Years ago, during my billboard-advertising selling days, I had the opportunity to participate in what was then called a market blitz. When a market—or, in this case, the city of Indianapolis and its surrounding communities—had a high availability of billboard advertising space, the district manager would "import" selling assistance in the form of salespeople from other areas to come in and blitz the market. The object for these imported mercenaries was to divide up the territory by geography and make cold calls on every business in the designated area. Goals were set for each salesperson, and an overall goal was established to reduce the number of available billboard space to a much more acceptable level. We had thirty days in which to accomplish this assignment while still managing our current customer base in our home market.

At that time, I was a sales associate in the Chicago metro territory. I was "asked" to get my current accounts in order and get ready to spend the next thirty days on the road working in Indianapolis. I was going to be part of the blitz to improve the advertising space occupancy rate in the Indianapolis market. Whether it was with long-term or short-term contracts, the object was to get some advertising on the available billboard space and do it fast. There would be an incentive of double the commission points for every sale made and the opportunity to count those points toward the year-end reward, which in those days was a week-long trip, a company-paid vacation to an exotic place somewhere in the world announced earlier in the year at the national sales meeting. Examples of those types of places were Hawaii, Australia, Hong Kong, and Italy, when a company sponsoring trips outside of the mainland United States was not only acceptable but was an anticipated perk to the selling job. I was fortunate enough to be rewarded with several company trips over the course of time as a billboard sales representative.

These trips were not only a great incentive and provided a huge stimulus for motivation to sell, it was also a great opportunity to meet and bond with fellow associates from across the country on a yearly basis. Of course, you could bring a significant other as your partner, fully paid for by the company as well. If you qualified for the trip, you were assured a great performance review and base salary raise. It was the perk that established your credibility within the organization. The focus throughout the year was on selling and making numbers, yet these trips really were about recognition and reward as a major support of management's pursuit to emphasize the importance of the people side of the business. They really cared about your efforts and wanted to ensure you were rewarded accordingly.

I believe these types of vacation incentives have been severely reduced in nature over the course of time and are now more of a business write-off in the form of a national meeting, complete with some form of training for those in attendance. It's not so much a sales incentive program, but more of a human resources function that recognizes achievements of people in other parts of the organization and not just the salespeople. This totally makes sense. All significant contributors should have an opportunity for reward and recognition, and their qualification for that type of incentive should be clearly outlined in performance appraisal goals and expectations. While the sales representatives generate the top-line revenue, the organization would not be what it is without the contributions from all dedicated, focused employees.

With that in mind, I read once long ago that nothing really happens in business until something is sold. And as I learned during my blitzing days, There Is No Finish Line to This Job. The effort required to sell is constant. There may be breaks in the action, but the intensity and pressure to perform is always there. In short sales cycle periods, a salesperson is truly only as good as their last sales cycle results. It's month to month, week to week, day to day; there really is no finish line. There is always something to sell and always another prospective buyer in the market. Those salespeople who make their living based on high commission and low base salary have an even greater requirement to perform. So, while the pressure exists for the sales team to perform, there are a plethora of preselling activities that are required in order to get the sales team and the company in a position to make a sale. Thereby the premise I read years ago is exactly that: old and outdated. A lot occurs in business before a sale is made.

Marketing, advertising, operations, logistics, and administration, whether online or on site, must be in place and functioning exceptionally for the sales team to do their job. And once the sale is made, the opportunities for customer service, follow-up, delivery, and tracking must all be in place and working appropriately to ensure repeat business. Support must be there for the team and the company to succeed.

The pressure to perform is much greater on the sales team than in any other department. If you disagree, then I applaud you for taking your job and contribution to the success of the company seriously. Oh, by the way several questions: Do you have a number on your back? Are you measured in your performance appraisal in metrics that are a direct result of the salespeople's effectiveness? Do you share in the success and the failures of your organization as a whole? If you work in an organization that truly takes a team approach to results by measuring your performance, perhaps in the form of a bonus as a shared function with the sales team's results, then I understand the pressure you have along with the sales team. There's a bit of incentive built in to support the sales team to be successful. You're not only doing your job because you want to perform above expectations, but you also want the organization to succeed so the willingness to help the sales team as necessary to succeed is ingrained in your daily routine. Seems obvious, right? Not necessarily.

Too often, I've seen the division that exists between the sales organization and support functions, which really tears at the heart of what a great organization should be and is an example of how careless companies operate. Call it jealousy, call it lacking in ownership, call it lacking in accountability—it doesn't really matter. If there is a division between how the sales team is measured and how other parts of the organization are rewarded, then the opportunity to finger point at a sales team's poor performance and not be held accountable in turn is a huge detriment to an organization. Everyone is the organization. Everyone is accountable. Everyone shares the responsibility to be a contributor toward the success of the organization. Compensation plans and award programs should reflect that accordingly.

With that in mind, the effort to succeed as a team requires effective communication, respect, cooperation, a commitment to excellence, and a complete understanding of dedication to ensure the job gets done. Those who fully engage in the process and are "all in" realize the importance of this direction as a foundation for building a solid team and an organization's culture. "We" takes the place of "they."

Simply put, we win together.

With that premise in mind, maximum effort from every individual in all parts of the organization is essential to deliver successfully. It is not only a message in a vision statement, but it also is a requirement and is measured and documented. It is a sense of culture. Those who believe in this commitment get to stay and share in the rewards. Those who have a "me first" attitude ("I'm not in sales; it's their fault") get to find a different organization. Thanks for playing. Move on.

As a sales manager in an organization, you have the authority, the positional power, and the right to demand other departments support your team's effort. The organization shares the ownership of the results. You have the say-so to engage other department leaders to instill upon them the mentality that seems to come naturally to those who choose sales as a career option.

Sales is not a nine to five job. Sales is a job where hours are dictated by the customer buying schedule. It's not too much to ask others in the organization share the There Is No Finish Line to This Job mentality for the benefit of the organization.

Getting others to share the premise requires you to utilize your persuasiveness, influence, and natural sales ability to make the case to your department peers as to why executing on this premise is best for all and for the overall good of the organization. Perhaps you work in an organization where this has already been established. Congratulations. Hold up your end of the bargain and contribute at a level that exceeds your coworker's expectations. If you have some selling to do to get others on the same page, take a logical features-advantage-benefits approach with your peers, and good things will happen. Show them why it makes sense for their teams to get on the same page as your team as far as supporting the sales effort for the benefit of the organization. Make them feel part of the team that takes on the front-line approach with customers. It will pay dividends in the long run.

As a wrap-up to the billboard sales blitz, we ended up selling enough contracts that amounted to thirty billboards in thirty days: amazingly successful, personally gratifying, and tremendously educational. We could not have achieved our selling goals without significant support from the other departments in our region. The success we had as a team was documented and presented as a staple in training exercises for many years to follow. Other markets utilized the blitz effort and team support strategy to improve their sales and reduce advertising space availability. We set the precedent for a life lesson. I learned that it takes a team effort to be successful in business, and when all involved share a common work ethic mentality, that is a tough combination to beat.

LESSON 17: WHAT GETS MEASURED GETS DONE

Do what you can with what you have where you are.
—Teddy Roosevelt

For optimum performance, concentrate efforts on the key performance indicators that have a direct positive effect on desired results.

Throughout my career, I've had the unique opportunity to work for several organizations that paid extreme close attention to the business's data points. In fact, a couple of these organizations paid so close attention to the business's data points that they were better at scorekeeping than they were at using the data to make good business decisions to drive growth. The focus was overly intense on how well the data could be gathered, analyzed, interpreted, presented, reviewed, and stored for future use (i.e., "year over year, quarter, month, day, hour, minute review"), as opposed to being enabled as a useful tool to increase sales. It is a major responsibility for management to review the business's data on a regular basis. But it is also a major responsibility of management to react to the data and implement necessary changes to stimulate growth. Placing way too much emphasis on having data as opposed to how to use it to make a positive impact really puts a crimp into those businesses in regard to developing and staying ahead of the competition.

I believe this paralysis by analysis comes about because it's a safe way for certain types of managers to spend the greater part of their day, as they believe they are contributing to the organization by spending time doing deep dives into data points. They put in a full day with the numbers, which in their minds is the job. The real aspect of a sales manager's job is to spend time coaching and developing salespeople. Building competency and confidence should be the sales manager's priority, yet I've seen it all too often in organizations that over emphasize the numbers, that the sales manager gets overly wrapped up in them and loses focus on the priority.

Now, I am all in favor of making data driven decisions. I fully support the concept taught to me years ago of "let the data direct the business." Being data informed is a critical aspect of a sales manager's repertoire and is supported by the fact that managers need to know their numbers as a part of being successful. But, more importantly, they need to know how to interpret the numbers and make sound business decisions based on what the numbers indicate to be able to keep the business moving forward, growing, attaining greater profitable revenue.

Certainly, I agree with having data analysts on board to crunch the numbers. Big data and its importance to growing a business depend on those people who have the skill set to identify key performance indicators, measure them effectively, and commit to changing the business according to what the numbers indicate.

For an example of how analyzing data to make business decisions is at the forefront of the business, all you need to do is look at Major League Baseball. Specifically, the story of the Oakland Athletics, as documented via the book *Moneyball*, by Michael Lewis, and the subsequent movie by the same name. The A's, via their general manager, Billy Beane, disrupted the traditional approach to drafting, trading for, trading away, and signing free agents based significantly upon data analysis. While Major League Baseball proved proficient at scorekeeping historical statistics, no team analyzed, interpreted, and implemented action based on what the data directed as the A's were able to do. They built a contending competitive team with the smallest payroll. They maximized efficiency and delivered expected results, much like a real business would strive to do. Oh, wait, they determined to consider themselves a business and used the data appropriately to drive results. They were action oriented.

One of the most important aspects of what the A's did, however, was to use the data to predict success. They were able to build models of potential outcomes via predictive analysis that no other team at the time had thought about doing. Or at least if they did, they didn't act on it to make the team better. The A's focused on predictive tendencies and used that information to their advantage. They figured out which key performance indicators had an impact on future success. They narrowed their focus to those specific KPIs that were more critical to results than the traditional plethora of scorekeeping data that MLB was so fond of using. In essence, the A's management executed on their strategy that a player's on-base percentage was a much more valuable data point and a much more reliable predictor of team success than traditional data points of home runs, runs batted in, and slugging percentages of individual players. This theory proved correct for the way the game was played in the early 2000s.

Fast-forward a few years, and every Major League Baseball team is using big data to drive business decisions. And while no team will abandon the emphasis on data analysis, several teams still rely on the human element to determine direction of their business decisions, mainly relying on past performance and a history of success as a measure of future continued success.

If you think that line of reasoning is enough to make decisions, then please help me understand why there are so many highly priced, overly priced ball players collecting big salaries and contributing at less than average performance standards? Examples are Jake Arrieta, Albert Pujols, Evan Longoria, Cole Hamels—all former All-Stars and highly productive players, all in the declining years of their baseball careers, yet still raking in the big bucks.

It will be interesting to see how starting pitcher Gerrit Cole fairs with the New York Yankees over the next few years. Cole signed a nine-year contract valued at $324 million. Unbelievable. That's an average annual value of $36 million. I wonder what data points the Yankees used to determine that this twenty-nine-year-old is worth that kind of money? Wins versus losses, innings pitched, earned run average, strikeouts—all these and most likely several more, yet in all the reading I did on this major contract, I didn't find one KPI that quenched my thirst for predictability of success. So, if the Yankees win the World Series in the next few years and Cole plays a major role in the success of their pitching staff, that will be the measure of the metric.

However, while I love baseball and its use of big data analysis to impact results, our focus here returns to our sales manager.

With all the available options for data gathering, analysis, interpretation, number crunching, and resources, how does a sales manager know what numbers on which to focus? How can a sales manager choose the right KPI on which to focus that will provide a predictive model of success?

The easy, traditional answer: sales results by representative based on selling cycle of the business. For example, let's say our sales cycle is on an eight-week reporting basis. Gather the data for that most recent time period, and then review each sales representative's performance during that eight-week period and make appropriate comparisons to prior performance. Look for trends, look for discrepancies, look for influencing factors. Interpret the data, and then make good business decisions regarding overall performance.

That is a very, very simplistic basic formula on which to build. It's traditional, just like Major League Baseball at one time, which was mired in a data analysis slump. It doesn't consider a bigger picture. It is narrowly focused on a microperiod in time. However, it's a start. But it's not an end, nor is it to be considered a foolproof method.

Here's why it's not the answer of answers. Because it is basic scorekeeping. It is focused on after-the-fact results. It misses the importance of the process data points. It misses out on what happened during the eight-week period from a standpoint of which significant KPI influenced the sales results…kind of like the A's figuring out on-base percentage was a better indicator of success than slugging statistics.

In order to get a better understanding of what influenced the sales representatives results for the eight-week period, the data-intelligent sales manager will focus on the KPI influencer that impacted—or, in better terms, delivered—results. The sales manager will use that significant influencer as a foundation for analyzing the data and determining future success.

For example:

| Sales Results Period March - April | | Period | Avg. Revenue | | | Presentations | Closing | Sales Per |
Representative	Total Sales Revenue	Customers	per Customer	Contacts	Presentations	Closed	Ratio	Closing
Rep A	$ 165,000.00	16	$ 10,312.50	55	36	16	44.4%	$ 644.53
Rep B	$ 160,000.00	14	$ 11,428.57	46	29	14	48.3%	$ 816.33
Rep C	$ 155,000.00	16	$ 9,687.50	60	33	16	48.5%	$ 605.47
Rep D	$ 120,000.00	8	$ 15,000.00	56	11	8	72.7%	$ 1,875.00
Rep E	$ 95,000.00	10	$ 9,500.00	42	18	10	55.6%	$ 950.00
Rep F	$ 85,000.00	7	$ 12,142.86	36	21	7	33.3%	$ 1,734.69
Total / Avg.	$ 780,000.00	71	$ 10,985.92	295	148	71	48.0%	$ 928.39

In looking at the basic sales results table above for the eight-week period, March through April, the sales representatives are ranked by their revenue contribution for the sales cycle.

A quick glance, and we see Rep A, Rep B, and Rep C lead the team in sales revenue and accounted for 61.5 percent of the total revenue. If we stop there and believe they are the most productive on the team, we are being just a bit short-sighted. We are only focusing on the scorekeeping aspect of the chart, not fully using the data to make managerial decisions. We can compare Rep A, Rep B, and Rep C with the "sluggers" from *Moneyball*. They hit home runs and bring in revenue for sure, but there's something wrong with their overall performance. They are leaving money on the table! They should be closing more sales based on the number of presentations they made during the period, and thereby should be producing more revenue than they delivered.

Whereby, in contrast, Rep D, with a closing ratio of 72.7 percent, is generating more than twice as much revenue per sale than the three sluggers...kind of like the ball player who has a much greater on-base percentage as being more valuable to the overall success of the team.

First, the direction here is to find out what is holding back Rep A, Rep B, and Rep C from closing more of their presentations, and most importantly, to find out what Rep D is doing so well to generate such a high closing ratio. This scenario presents a training opportunity for all the team.

Secondly, we need to get Rep D to increase the number of presentations per sales period. With just four more presentations per sales period and with a similar closing ratio as currently being generated, Rep D would deliver the same overall sales revenue as Rep A at $165,000.

| $ | 165,000.00 | 11 | $ 15,000.00 | 56 | 15 | 11 | 73.3% | $ 1,363.64 |

So, while the results for the eight-week cycle speak for themselves as far as revenue, the real questions to try and answer are: What activities drove that revenue? What activities, if increased, would drive additional revenue? And most importantly, are we measuring and monitoring the correct KPIs that would influence the sales team to not only be aware they are being measured in this regard, but would also provide a stimulus to get them to increase sales?

Our example is basic and doesn't consider the skill set or seniority of the sales team. Nor does it provide any detail on extenuating circumstances like territory changes or customer scenarios that may impact results. Yet it does give us a reason to think differently at how we look at the team. Should each rep have a minimum number of contacts or presentations they need to make each month? Maybe. Based on skill set, territory, customer base, and other factors, having a dedicated requirement on these activities may be the measurement we seek to drive additional sales.

All I am saying here is to spend some time looking for the lead activities that have a positive impact on the desired results. Once identified, be sure the team understands why that KPI is being measured and monitored, and how it will be beneficial to both the representative and for the organization once adhered to accordingly.

Think of it this way. If you want to look better, feel better, improve your overall attitude and perhaps even impact your emotional intelligence in a positive manner, you simply don't just look in the mirror every day and hope for the best. No, you increase and improve upon the activities that have an impact on the desired results you seek. Perhaps you increase your exercise routine, improve your eating habits by adding more vegetables and eliminating sugar, spend a few minutes each day writing in your journal only positive thoughts, read a motivational article every day, and take the time to communicate with a friend who has the same motivations in mind. These are the items to help keep score. These are the items that, when measured and monitored, will have an impact on the results you want to attain. You are measuring the activities that drive productivity.

It can be the same in sales management. To improve sales results, look at your data points, and figure out which KPI activity has a direct impact on the results you seek. If you do this by individual sales representative, you will not only learn more about the overall business, but you will have another teaching-training-coaching opportunity for each of the representatives. Keep track, measure, monitor these KPI activities, and provide regular feedback to the team in this regard. Show them examples of how improvements in the KPI activities generates improvements in sales results. Then be sure to congratulate each one who achieves both KPI activity achievement and overall sales goal achievement. This approach will pay dividends.

LESSON 18: LEAD EFFECTIVE MEETINGS, AND STOP WASTING YOUR SALESPEOPLE'S TIME

The true art of memory is the art of attention.

I'm going to make this lesson learned brief and to the point:

If not managed appropriately, meetings can be the single most waste of a salesperson's time.

If not managed appropriately, meetings can have the single most adverse effect on productivity for your organization.

Whether you agree or disagree with the prior two statements, I am sure you will reflect upon a time that you were saddled in a sales meeting for an inordinate amount of time. You most likely became bored with the meeting's presenter and content and couldn't wait for the drawn-out session to end. Your thoughts wandered to your email, the phone calls you needed to return, what you were having for lunch. *Is it my turn to pick up the kids from daycare? Oh no, not another PowerPoint. Why can't people just log in on time for the conference call? Please do not provide hard copies of your presentation; we're supposed to be paperless, remember? Can't I just get back to doing my work? I have customers I need to call. Every minute I'm stuck in here is another minute lost from my day.*

Am I getting closer to convincing you with my opening statements? No? Then how about this?

Have you ever led a meeting where you were asked to present material in which you did not have complete understanding or control over its contents? The corporate office asked you to "roll out" something they needed to be addressed with the sales teams across the country? Ever get into a situation in which your audience did not see you as credible? The presentation was a waste of time and could have been done online? Ever have your sales team question the roll-out material as not being legitimate, as the home office failed to do their homework and only addressed the situation partially?

Those of you who experienced this type of situation know exactly what I mean. Those who have yet to experience this situation are lucky you haven't had the pleasure. Your day is coming. Enjoy.

I'm not saying to eliminate all meetings, but you and I both know that not all meetings are productive. Some, in fact, are a huge waste of time and effort. Some do more damage than good to the morale of the sales team. In recognizing the amount of nonproductive time employees spend in meetings, some organizations instituted rules that meetings can be held only on certain days and are limited in length to less than one hour or so. I'm not sure that's the answer to increase communications. I'm sure that's not the secret to improving employee productivity.

My focus in this lesson learned is centered around the sales manager and the sales team and how to make time spent in a sales meeting productive for both entities.

The concept about having sales meetings and their usefulness depends on the situation at hand. New managers, new teams, major changes in the organization structure, new products to review, new customers to discuss, new operational issues to address, forecasts being due, budgets and quotas being assigned, compensation plan changes, and performance review process are just some of the items that perhaps may require a meeting with the team. Those are potential topics that may require a special session. They are important topics and need to be addressed. My opinion in this regard is to look for the most efficient and least time-consuming way to present these special meeting topics to your team. Do not bog them down from their sales responsibility. Make these special meeting presentations as least intrusive to the salespeople's time as possible. If possible, partner with another sales manager if that's what it takes to get these special meetings out to the broader audience in a more efficient manner. Do whatever it takes in this regard within reason and legitimacy in your company's environment, and then move on to the business at hand.

For this lesson learned, I want to shift attention to the weekly sales meeting.

I am not opposed to conducting regular weekly sales meetings. I am in favor of facilitating well-prepared, organized, and effectively delivered weekly sales meetings.

There is a time and place for conducting regular sales meetings, whether they be done virtually or face to face. Sales meetings provide an opportunity for the team to touch base, get questions answered, be motivated, "feel" the culture (especially for those who work remotely), and be informed of new developments and ideas; they, of course, should be addressed to meet the needs of the team. "What's in it for me?" is an age-old yet still effective position for a sales manager to take when preparing the upcoming sales meeting. The salespeople will want to know if this meeting is worth their time.

With that in mind, here is the basic, pure, simple, and always relevant outline for any sales manager to use with the sales team in any weekly sales meeting. The outline covers five major points for delivery and, once implemented effectively, will keep the meeting moving and address the attention-span shortcomings of any participants. I'm not saying salespeople have short attention spans. I'm just saying the average adult attention span is somewhere around seven minutes. Salespeople may be on the downside of that stat.

I will attest to this fact: salespeople would rather be somewhere else than in a sales meeting.

First and foremost: Ditch the PowerPoint. Why? Read the next point.

Second: The sales manager will facilitate a weekly sales meeting *discussion*; no slides are needed once everyone knows the meeting format and expectations.

Third: The weekly sales meeting discussion will include the following items:

Published agenda

Discussion of business data points

Recognition

Training

Question and answer

Fourth: The weekly sales meeting will start promptly at the designated time and finish prior to or right at the designated ending time.

Published agenda. Ever been invited to a meeting in which the facilitator neglects to send out an agenda prior to the meeting? You know the meeting topic because it's on the calendar invite, but you don't know what's in store for discussion or whether you need to be prepared for potential items outside of the meeting topic. Publishing an agenda does not have to be elaborate. It just needs to provide the participants with an idea of what is going to be discussed, in what order, and if the facilitator has items which require more in-depth contributions from the participants. Publishing an agenda shows the participants you care about their time and will conduct a well-organized meeting. People who know what to expect will also have a better understanding of what to prepare for the meeting. I suggest sending out the agenda at least twenty-four hours prior to the meeting to provide enough notice for participants to prepare.

Discussion of business data points. The sales manager should provide a point-in-time summary of the team sales results in comparison to budget. Individual weekly, monthly, and quarterly expectations compared to budget may be summarized by individual salespeople. To save time in this regard, perhaps there is a sales report that can be seen online to visualize how everyone is contributing to the team results. Forecasts for the upcoming period may also be topics of discussion, with the sales manager providing the team a progress report based on input from the individual salespeople. Discussing the numbers is a critical aspect of the weekly sales meeting in two regards. It allows for all engaged in the meeting to know just where they stand and that you, as the sales manager, take the achievement of hitting budget seriously. It also provides an opportunity as foundation for the next agenda item.

Recognition. Every sales meeting should provide an opportunity to recognize a member or several members of the team for their contributions to the organization. While individuals achieving their quotas and the team achieving budget are items for consideration, please look for other non-numbers-related scenarios that are perfect opportunities to reward and recognize people in front of their peers. Perhaps one of the salespeople received a testimonial from a customer. Maybe the sales assistant put in extra hours to help a salesperson with a challenging proposal. Maybe there is a new member on the team who recently completed their training or orientation period. It could be as simple as saying thank you to every member of the team for their dedicated effort in support of the team goals. Always look to recognize individuals and, when possible, the team. Maybe you have a floating award that goes from team member to team member each week; the person who earned the teammate of the office award for helping out, being positive at all times, promoting the core values of the company and is consistent is delivering prompt efficient and courteous service to coworkers. While I am focused on the formality of the meeting, it is OK to have fun in the meeting. The recognition part of the agenda can be a perfect opportunity to lighten up the meeting.

Training. Delivering a weekly training topic can be a bit tricky. The topic itself must be relevant, informative, and delivered in a short amount of time. If a guest presenter is invited to the meeting, the tendency is for the presenter to dominate the meeting. The presentation then becomes just that: a presentation with no opportunity for discussion or feedback. No one wants to be lectured to in this regard. The training topic must be one in which the sales team perceives the benefit of its usefulness in how it directly relates to their job. Thereby, if appropriate, it may be best served to have one of the salespeople deliver the training topic in this format: "Here's a challenge I had with a customer, and here's how I handled the situation." Or "Here's a challenge I have with a customer, and what are your suggestions as to how I should handle the situation?" Getting the team to participate makes for a more discussion-based meeting. Having them assist in figuring out the answer to the challenging situation also improves the skill set and problem-solving ability of the team. The sales manager may also take this opportunity to propose a customer scenario to the team and ask for feedback on how it should best be handled. Simply stated, this is an exercise whereby everyone learns from each other.

Question and answer. Depending on the length of the meeting, there should be a few minutes left to allow the salespeople to ask a question or two in general terms for the benefit of the team specifically addressed by the sales manager for response. More detailed questions should be saved for a one-on-one opportunity with the sales manager. There may be an item of interest that, when addressed, will provide the team with a motivation, an incentive, and information that, when applied, will help them be more productive. This closing section of the meeting also allows for words of wisdom. Leave the meeting on a positive note. Provide a motivational saying. Tell a brief story about someone else's success. Mention a news item that leaves people feeling good. Find something that will assist in building their confidence. And most importantly, thank them for their time, effort, dedication, and commitment to getting the job done with the best interests of the company in mind while servicing the customer base in a superior manner. Always thank them sincerely. You know you are doing a good job when they tell you thank you in return for your attention to them.

My final thoughts on weekly sales meetings: The meeting is your meeting with your team. It is not your boss's meeting.

It is not your boss's boss's meeting. It is not an opportunity for anyone to come in and hijack your time with the salespeople. It is your accountability and your responsibility. Most important is the premise that you will get out of the meeting the same level of productivity in which you put forth the effort to prepare and deliver the meeting. This is a one-for-one exchange. Appropriate effort on your behalf delivers the desired return on expectations. Take your meeting and meeting preparation seriously, and the return on investment will be well warranted.

If all else fails and you are struggling to facilitate a weekly sales meeting for whatever reason, or maybe you just don't want to have a meeting, cancel the meeting, and go make sales calls. And be sure to tell everyone who was supposed to attend that you are canceling the meeting to go make sales calls.

You just might come across some material for your next sales meeting...and maybe even make a sale in doing so!

LESSON 19: IF IT'S NOT IN WRITING, THEN IT DOESN'T EXIST

It's important for people to know what you stand for.
It's equally important that they know what you won't stand for.
—Mary Waldrip

In interviewing salespeople throughout the years, I always asked them to describe what they thought would be the top three characteristics of a person who would be successful in the job for which they were interviewing. Then I would ask them to name their top three characteristics and how those relate to the job for which they were interviewing. You would be surprised at how many of those individuals named characteristics that didn't match the ones they just said of people who would be successful in the job. I mean seriously. These two direct questions are softballs. They should be easily addressed by anyone who is serious about the job interview, especially a salesperson, who should recognize the obvious. Relate the answer to the subject matter, and then describe how you fit the bill.

It should be a piece of cake.

Yet while I would get answers to the first question such as being persistent, being a good communicator, having an outgoing personality, being organized, and being able to relate to different people, those same interviewees would provide totally different characteristics for the second part of the question. Some of those answers included being hardworking, intelligent, creative, willing to learn, and adaptable. OK, those are not bad, but you would still have to provide me with an example of each of those traits for me to believe that you are hardworking, intelligent, creative, willing to learn, and adaptable. My favorite answer from a candidate was "I like to have fun at work." OK, yes, we certainly want to have fun at work, but that answer alone is not going to convince me that you will take the job seriously, let alone get you hired in the first place.

It was difficult for me to understand how ill prepared some people were for the interview process, and certainly those who could not see past the relationship between those two softball questions really befuddled me. They came in cold and left colder. They hadn't prepared and did not think through the situation. They hadn't visualized the interview, anticipated questions, or seen themselves answering in a manner that related their skill set to the job at hand. They hadn't taken the time to write down any possible responses to potential questions. They weren't smart enough to take it seriously. Maybe they were too smart for their own good. They weren't hired.

On the contrary to those lackluster candidates, I've also had the pleasure of interviewing numerous outstanding, well-prepared, and highly engaging sales candidates. Those people did their homework and easily addressed the softball questions by providing a detailed description of who they were and how their characteristics would relate to those currently successful in the job. Much better. They at least put themselves in a position to be considered for hire. I sincerely believe those candidates took the time to write out potential questions and answers and reviewed the possibilities more than just once in their collective minds.

I also sincerely believe that putting things in writing provides foundation for learning. Why do students take notes in class? Why do people take notes in meetings? Why do salespeople write down key information from customers? Why do people use their iPads and laptops and cell phones and other electronic devices to capture the key elements of any meeting? It's obvious. To provide a reference point. To learn. To assist in remembering. To study for the test. To provide follow-up communication to the team. To document.

Yes, to document.

Now, I'm not writing here about your upcoming trip to the grocery store and the list you compiled to shop for your groceries. (Although it begs the question of whether you or your partner use a grocery list. Perhaps you use notes in your cell phone instead of the old-fashioned write-it-down grocery list?) Maybe you are not a list maker at all. Maybe you shop on impulse alone. Maybe you don't shop at all and just eat out a lot. Maybe you shop online and have all your groceries available for pick up or delivery.

For me, if I don't have it written down, it doesn't exist. Yes, I am a list maker. Regardless if it's for the grocery store, chores around the house, or for tasks at work, I write it down. I make a list. I work off the list to stay organized. I use the list to measure my productivity and gain a sense of accomplishment. I feel good about creating the list because I've identified the things I need to do, and I feel even better when I can cross things off the list because I've completed the work. And one other important thing: *I write to document.*

Have you ever been in a situation whereby a dispute between two employees in your stead came to your desk for a determination of understanding? Have you ever been in a situation whereby the performance appraisal you delivered is not agreed to nor signed off by the receiving employee? Have you ever had to prove your support or opposition to a company directive that later turned out to be for the benefit of or to the detriment of the welfare of the organization?

Have you ever thought how important it is to have a paper trail?

Have you ever thought to yourself, "I better not put that in writing"?

Have you ever thought to yourself, "I need to put that in writing"?

Have you ever said, "Can I get that in writing?"

Have you ever thought how important it is for you to follow up in writing with an employee after a one-on-one meeting, especially a meeting that involved a corrective action discussion?

Have you ever sent an email that you later regretted sending?

Right now, you are thinking about those questions and reminding yourself about those types of scenarios. You've been there, done that, lived it, experienced it, confirmed the reality.

Regardless of the seriousness or the liability, you know there are times when you wished you had the paper. You wish you could show the document that others signed off on or that you were provided approval by your manager to do something. You wish you had kept better notes of discussions you had with "that employee," the one that just keeps turning up like a bad penny and is on the path to either being terminated or rewarded with a settlement package. You wish you had documented the sales meetings with the team because now you need to prove that you provided training to the employee who complained to HR about their performance appraisal results and that their less-than-acceptable rating is due in part to inadequate training. You wish you had done a better job in writing down your observations of your salespeople in discussions with their customers.

Not to worry. You can start building the paper trail now. Get out the laptop and start the note-taking process. Make it a plan of action that you will do a better job in writing down the details that you deem important and that will help you be a better manager.

And for a few others out there...

You wish you hadn't sent that email. You wish you had written the email just to vent, get it off your chest, let out some emotional steam, and then hit the delete button instead of the send button. You wish you didn't get into a situation where your manager is questioning your managerial effectiveness. You wish you didn't put your opinion in writing to the HR manager about that certain situation between two fellow employees.

You wish that you didn't have to wish.

Don't worry; this too shall pass. Things always work out for the best. No matter how bad you perceive the situation, it's not as bad as you think. People make mistakes; no one is perfect. Stop beating yourself up; it's not worth the effort. Believe me, I know this from experience.

And then document the hell out of what you know is right.

Too often, the blame for a poor outcome rests with the manager who fails to engage in the art of appropriate documentation. Whether it be a discussion with an employee or a meeting with your manager, take the time to write down the facts. Leave the interpretation or opinion out; just document the actual. And do so immediately after the meeting. Do not wait until the next day. Your recollection and ability to play back the discussion in your mind will be at its peak immediately after the meeting. This is a great practice in which to engage after conducting an interview. Document your notes on the candidate immediately.

It might not seem important at the time, yet it will become critical in the future. You will have the documentation to support your position or decision, refresh your memory on how that certain discussion occurred, and most importantly, be able to dispute false accusations from others who may have a different interpretation of how the conversation went down. If you don't have the documentation to support your position, you don't have a leg on which to stand. It becomes your word versus their word.

Regardless of outcome of the situations and whether the manager is proved correct or the counter part is proved correct, why take chances? Why not do your own diligence to protect yourself? I guarantee the people who are your best friends in human resources will become innocent bystanders and third-party, neutral observers if you are intertwined in a situation without appropriate documentation defending your position. They will turn on you as fast as they welcomed you to the organization; they are just doing their jobs. It is up to you to do yours as well in this regard to protect your own best interests.

A final word of caution: Be careful what you put in writing and with whom you share the documentation. The real secret to compiling excellent documentation is to know the difference between what to document and what to leave best alone. Think it through. Can it be used against me later? Should I copy others in authority positions to ensure my intentions are understood and my position covered? Is this the type of documentation I want to hold for my eyes only?

Let's not leave this lesson learned with a negative perspective on documentation. Do not get into a thought process that is defensive and suspicious. Stay positive and determined. Do your job appropriately, as most of your documented discussions will be used for great things like providing an outstanding performance appraisal and recommending a promotion for a fellow employee. Appropriate documentation of your own performance can become a very useful tool if you are asked to provide input on your own appraisal. It may also come in handy if you are leaving the company and wish to prove your performance in the interview process with your potential new employer.

You may be thinking at this point should I have separate files of documentation and keep them outside of the office...in my own personal privacy. It is best that you answer that question for yourself. Only you can determine to go that route, so you should understand the risks that go along with taking that approach, and it may be against your company policy. So think it through.

For me, I'll keep writing out my grocery list, my chores, my goals. I'll avoid too much impulse buying outside of what's on the list. I'll get things done. I'll measure my accomplishments against the things I want to achieve this year. I'll document my customer discussions. I'll keep to the facts and stay positive in those discussions. I'll build relationships and earn trust with my business associates. I'll know where I stand and I'll be prepared for any potential differences of opinion, or differences of direction or disagreement.

I'll be in a much better position because I'll have it in writing...and thereby it will exist.

LESSON 20: PLAY TO YOUR STRENGTHS, YET SEEK TO IMPROVE

*Challenges make you discover things about
yourself that you never really knew.*
—Cicely Tyson

One of my mentors during my years at 3M Company was a gentlemen named Greg Linnerooth. I will always be indebted to Greg for guiding my career at 3M, but most importantly, I am grateful to him for promoting me to the sales training manager position for the outdoor advertising business, which he led as its vice president of marketing and sales.

As the sales training manager, I was responsible for three major initiatives:

1) Build and facilitate an in-house training program for newly hired sales representatives.
2) Travel as often as possible to conduct field training sessions for current representatives.

3) Take a leadership role in managing the National Sales Meeting for the division.

The position was national in scope, reported directly to Greg, and held a visible level of legitimate authority among my peer sales managers, mostly due to Greg's emphasis on the importance of training. He needed a person who knew the business from a salesperson's and sales manager's perspective, among other skill sets, and while there were several other candidates for the job, Greg offered me the position.

Being the only sales trainer for a business that, at its peak, had roughly five hundred sales representatives in various major markets across the country was going to be a challenge, let alone the fact that I was replacing a well-respected senior-level trainer who was retiring from the position. It also required relocation to Chicago, and while Chicago was my hometown, it was going to be a major transition for my wife, Robin, who had been born and raised in New Orleans and had lived there all her life, as well as our one-year-old son, Christopher, and Robin's nine-year-old daughter, Carin. Not to mention that it was also a difficult transition for Robin's parents, who also had been born and raised in New Orleans and had lived there all their lives; Robin was their only daughter and Carin and Chris their only grandchildren. Oh, and another thing: if I didn't accept the job, I would have to find other options either within 3M or outside of the company, as the New Orleans office that I managed was going to be consolidated with another office. A little pressure, a little stress, a little bit of a challenge, both personally and professionally.

Fortunately, as is the case with many things in life, it all worked out. From the family side, maybe Grammie and Gramps didn't get to see their grandchildren as often as they would have liked, but they always had a place to visit in Naperville, Illinois (in the summertime, mostly), and we had a place to visit in Saint Rose, Louisiana, year round. Our second son, Corey, was born several months after our move, adding to the excitement. Robin and Carin both proved to be real troupers, adjusting to the coldest climate and most densely populated area in which they had ever lived. The food was good, the schools were great, and I am proud to say all three of the children graduated from the same high school, before moving on to different colleges so we planted our roots and adapted accordingly. I renewed old friendships, and we all made new friends as well. And work was more than just a job.

Greg took me under his wing and opened my eyes to a bigger picture of the business that I had previously never really seen. He provided me the opportunity to get ingrained in the business via support, direction, leadership, and friendship. I realized he had a stake in the game and wanted me to be successful, since he was the one who gave me a chance at the sales training manager position. His reputation was a little bit on the line as well, subject to me being a good fit for the role and whether I could be "his" guy to help push his agenda through the organization. I like to think years later that not only did I prove to be a great sales trainer, but

I also learned about being a great facilitator, thanks to Greg. It was easy to be "his" guy because he was so easy to get along with, was a fun person to work for and with, and always placed people first in any situation. He ran the business based on respect for those who worked with him and, in return, rewarded those who maintained that same perspective.

But the one thing that really stood out about Greg that helped me become a great facilitator was his ability to tell a story. Greg was a tremendous storyteller. Whether it was in a room of over one thousand employees at a national sales meeting, or at a dinner at his house with eight of the newly hired salespeople as part of their training class, or at one of the 3M customer retreats at Wonewok Resort in northern Minnesota, Greg could hold an audience like no one I had ever seen. His ability to relate a story was uncanny. He could tell a story in such a way that he made you feel as if you were part of the story itself. How he acquired this ability, I don't know. All I do know is that he used it to his benefit on numerous occasions. He recognized this storytelling ability as one of his key strengths and played to it religiously. It worked tremendously to his benefit with any audience.

If I tried to relate the stories to you that I remember, it just wouldn't be the same. I would not do them justice in writing. They are the kind of stories you must hear in person to fully appreciate.

Nevertheless, I can remember asking Greg to tell the story to my new hire sales training classes about the sales representative who worked for him years ago who was always at the top of the sales leaders list—the same sales representative who admitted later to changing and increasing several customers' order-form quantities to increase his sales volume. You can imagine the outcome of that story. Yet the way Greg would tell it and describe the details would have us all laughing hysterically. Or the one about his high school baseball coach who, in situations where his pitcher was being hit hard in a game, would make a visit to the pitching mound and "coach" up his pitcher by telling him the obvious...that he was being hit hard and needed to do better. Not much coaching going on there, but certainly an example of what not to do as a coach. Greg would then take this and relate it to how a good coach offers encouragement via a more in-depth approach to a difficult situation.

But the story I like most that Greg would tell, relates best to this lesson learned about playing to your strengths. It is about the Chinese table tennis team.

As a point of reference, the Chinese dominate the sport of table tennis. Since its inception into the summer Olympic games in 1988, China owns the sport winning fifty-three medals, twenty-eight of thirty-two possible gold, with their nearest competitor being South Korea, with eighteen overall medals going into the 2020 Olympics. There are a variety of reasons why China dominates this event and this sport overall. First, table tennis or Ping-Pong (or Pingpang qiu) is the country's national sport, declared as such in the 1950s by then-leader Chairman Mao. Second, China has the largest number of table tennis players in the world. The pool of talent from which they can choose is unmatched by any other country. Third, the Chinese maintain an extremely rigorous and definitive training program, as is the case with all Chinese athletic programs, but table tennis training in China is unprecedented. The competition to earn a roster spot for their national team is ridiculously intense. Fourth, while other countries work on strategy, tactics, and technique, the Chinese concentrate on the basics of perfecting their forehand and backhand shots. They play to their strengths. They promote the basics and work at it like no other country's players are able to.

Greg could tell the story about how the Chinese spent hours and hours working on their forehand serve and forehand return and then spend hours and hours working on their backhand return, all with the intent to remind the sales team that working on the basics and perfecting those characteristics in sales would lead to great success. He reminded us as salespeople to learn the basics and then play to our strengths. Challenge yourself in areas of deficiency, but always, always, always hone your selling skills around the foundation of sales in order to exceed the customer's expectations in all situations.

This line of thinking is solid and one that I took to heart in my role as a sales trainer. I wish to this day I could tell a story like Greg could, but I knew at the time that was not my forte. I've since become a lot better in that regard based on having to facilitate, present, and speak at training sessions, meetings, and convocation ceremonies over the years.

As a rookie sales trainer, I did have going for me the experience of having been a successful sales representative earning Commander's Club, the highest-ranking award for a 3M outdoor salesperson at the time. I had the knowledge of the job inside and out when it came to "how" to present outdoor advertising to a customer. As a sales manager, I learned the 3M way and spent numerous hours in onsite training classes at 3M's main campus in St. Paul, Minnesota. I also had an outstanding organizational skill set that I used to build a three-week comprehensive training program for our new hires that was detailed, engaging, and fun at the same time. Those who took it seriously would learn how to sell outdoor advertising space. And while it was still up to them to implement what they learned I gave them a great starting point. I spent more time traveling between 3M offices in a variety of states than I care to remember but used that opportunity to gain strength as a "road warrior." Getting out of the office spending time working with reps in the field added to my credibility and helped me stay up to date with current customers. An easy trap for a trainer in which to fall into is to become irrelevant by being a classroom teacher out of the flow of business. Greg ensured I would stay up to date and relevant by keeping me on the road as a requirement of job expectations.

I was playing to my strengths of knowledge, experience, organizational skills, credibility, loyalty, and my complete commitment to the company and our service. I was sold on 3M and outdoor advertising in general, and those strengths played well for me during my training classes.

I owe a lot of my ability as a facilitator of those training classes to Greg as he took me out of my comfort zone and put me in front of customers, peers, executives, home office management, company guests, and outside company representatives as often as possible to hone my skills. I learned to make facilitating and presenting one of my strengths because I was able to practice without the fear of making a fool of myself thanks to Greg's confidence in me. Presenting in front of a customer in a one on one selling situation is one thing. Standing up in front of over one thousand fellow 3M employees to open the national sales meeting, first speech of the day, first person on the docket, first person with all eyes focused on, is a totally different experience, one that I can look back on and be grateful for having the opportunity.

Whether or not you have identified your significant strengths, I suggest you take the time to really engage in this regard by asking your peers, representatives, coworkers, and superiors for their input. List what you think are your strengths. Ask them what they think your strengths are. Ask them what they would like to see you do less. Ask them what they would like to see you do more. Start doing this; stop doing this. The exercise will assist in determining how others perceive your contributions measured in your strengths. It may also identify areas that present a challenge and present an opportunity for you, once acknowledged and accepted, to improve your skill set.

In recognizing deficiencies, you may consider having someone on your team who can make up for an area in which you would like to getter better. For example, suppose math and data gathering, analysis, and interpretation are not your strong suit. You would much rather engage customers and people in general than spend time crunching numbers. Well, keep playing to your strength by being the best you can be during those people opportunities, and find someone who can assist you with the numbers. It's OK to seek help. You can't be everything to everyone. It's not a sign of weakness to ask for help. It's just the opposite. It shows you care enough to want to get better and learn in an area that perhaps is not your strong suit. The willingness to learn from others is a significant strength. Play it out.

One last thought: When playing to your strengths, you do something else that goes a long way toward being successful. You are keeping it simple. You are keeping it real. You are being yourself at your best. You are not trying to be something other than who you really are. I believe you should challenge yourself to continually improve, yet at the same time, recognize what got you to where you are. Most likely your current level of success is based on a solid core skill set. You are unique in that regard because it's you. Stick to it. Play to your strengths. Be the best you can be by using your strengths to exceed expectations.

At the same time, it's imperative to stretch yourself and challenge yourself to get better, to build on your strengths while tackling a shortcoming. I encourage you to pick an area on which to improve and go for it with full vim and vigor. Keep working at it until you reach a level of satisfaction and consistency. Then perhaps choose another area on which to improve and keep adding skill sets to your strengths. Over time, via continuous improvement, continuous learning, you will have added additional core strengths to your repertoire. You become much more valuable and marketable when you take the approach of continuous improvement and make good on that effort. No one-trick ponies here. You become more well-rounded, polished, and confident and can carry yourself with a new self-esteem. You continue to grow intellectually and present yourself with greater dignity, and others recognize you for the investment in which you made.

If you're not one already, you may even become a better storyteller in the process.

Thanks again, Greg.

LESSON 21: YOUR CUSTOMERS WILL GET BETTER WHEN YOU GET BETTER

---

*The one thing worse than a quitter is
the one who is afraid to begin.*

In teaching a graduate sales management class as an adjunct faculty member, I facilitated an exercise in which I would ask the students to tell me about their customers. Mind you, this was a sales management class, so many of my students were current or former sales representatives, marketing types, and customer service representatives, so the topic had a comfortable input opportunity and would resonate with the class.

The intent of the discussion was to explore customer scenarios in depth and address the question "Is the customer, always right?" yet I wanted to start the process with a little foundation. I believe a bit of self-reflection sometimes gets to the point quicker and opens the door for further understanding.

When I would ask the question, in a direct form, "Tell me about your customers," the immediate responses would be along these lines:

Oh, my customers are great. Without them, I wouldn't be able to pay my bills.

I love my customers; we've built a great relationship over the years.

My customers view me as a partner, so there's a lot of respect there, and they realize we are problem-solving together.

All fine and dandy. Perfect world. Love those customers. Where would we be without them?

Then there would be a few comments like this:

At times, my customers can be demanding; after all, they are charged with protecting their company's best interests.

I understand if my customers have conflicting priorities that upset my travel schedule. I just wish they would give me some advance notice if they are going to cancel an appointment.

Sometimes, my customers will call after hours or on the weekends, and if I don't respond immediately, they can get irate.

OK, a little bit of reality is setting in. Not all rainbows and butterflies. Savvy customers protecting their business interests.

Then there would be several comments along these lines:

Yes, those darn customers can be so demanding. They want increased discounts that aren't in line with their contract terms.

Sometimes they want privileged information regarding their competitors' contracts since my company does business with numerous organizations in their industry. They want to be sure their contract rates are less than what their competition is paying. They put me in a very awkward position. They demand delivery of my product on dates when they know we can't meet those demands just to see if I will cave in on my price.

My customers flat-out don't see me as a solution, just a necessary means to justify their intents. In fact, they could care less about me; they only care about meeting their needs.

What starts out as a discussion about how great customers are and how mutual respect between the salesperson and the customer provides a foundation for problem-solving and partnerships, ends up deteriorating to a discussion about numerous negative perspectives of customers and the challenges they present in the sales process.

Can't live with them, can't live without them. I wish they would just be easier with which to work.

To which I would provide a simple yet meaningful comment about understanding the intent of learning to be a professional salesperson and to make one's sales life a little bit easier: Your Customers Will Get Better When You Get Better. I apply this to both the individual and the organization. It simply means that if you make the investment to improve your individual skill set and your organization's buying process, you are more likely to deliver an improved customer experience.

Too often, we view our own challenges as being caused by those with whom we are working. Those darn customers just don't see it from my point of view. They don't understand the issues at hand and don't really care if I can't deliver to their demands.

Well, welcome to reality. Those darn customers are the reason why you are in business, and without them, you don't have a business.

Question one: When was the last time you invested in yourself to improve your product knowledge, communications skills, or negotiating skills; took a professional sales training course; or spent time listening and learning to gain expertise, respect, and credibility? If it's been a while, I suggest you get into the learning mode. Regardless of how long you've been selling or have been leading as a sales manager, the opportunity for improvement is always present. Take a fresh approach to the cliché "learn something new every day" by investing in yourself as a lifelong learner. While tangible items come and go, education is one thing that can never be taken away from you.

As a sales manager, your investment in yourself is also an investment in your sales team. You have a responsibility to them that centers on your ability to help them do their jobs better. It sounds simple, but in fact it is very challenging. They expect you to be coach, mentor, leader, sales guru, and confidant, among other things. They have expectations that you are looking out for their best interests and in turn are consistently working in that regard by improving your skill set as a manager. You owe it to them.

Question 2: When was the last time your organization looked internally at your selling process and especially looked at the customer buying process from your customer's point of view? Yes, mapping out the customer journey is a tedious and grueling exercise, but one that, if done correctly, will open your eyes to disconnects and dysfunctional aspects in your quest to provide an exceptional customer experience.

Exceptional customer experience should be the norm, regardless of the business. Organizations that make an investment in their employees and build on the premise that your customers will get better when you get better are placing themselves in a position of strength. They are paying attention to what really matters in sales: the customer's interaction with the business. Ensuring that the organization has a customer-centric, customer-focused buying process is at the core of the sales experience. It provides foundation for any and all points forward. Taking the time to map out this process from your customer's point of view will provide insight and opportunity. Once identified, options become available for continuous improvement.

That continuous improvement applies on an individual basis as well. Lifelong learning is one thing but having truly engaged sales representatives requires a passion for improvement. I'm a firm believer that people get into the sales business because they like to help people and they realize how personally satisfying it is to help others satisfy a need.

With that in mind, I encourage you to spend a little time on yourself and your process. Building an exceptional customer experience begins with you and in having an appreciation for how important every customer is to your business. When they see a fully invested, fully engaged sales representative who owns a customer-focused sales and buying process, most people can't help but be better customers, based on their satisfaction with the experience you delivered.

BONUS LESSON LEARNED: BASIC PRINCIPLES FOR INTERACTIONS WITH YOUR MANAGER

1) Try your best to make your manager look good in difficult situations, yet always hold true to your convictions, and do not compromise your integrity.

2) Do not give your manager any work to do; instead, offer to assist in challenges that others would rather not attempt.

3) Avoid arguing with your manager; however, tactfully express your opinion as needed to make your point.

4) It serves no purpose to antagonize your manager in meetings. Seek to provide appropriate support and encouragement to get your message across.

5) It's an embarrassment for both you and your manager if you correct your manager in front of his or her manager. Instead, use your sense of humor to ensure respect and exactness.

6) Think twice before sending a response with a correction to your manager's email spelling errors. Spell check can handle that for you.

7) It's unproductive to waste your manager's time on trivial items. Make every effort to maximize time spent for both of you.

8) Never send your manager an email suggesting how he or she should manage or do their job better, unless you have another job lined up.

9) Avoid leaving out the details you think may be unimportant when having a difficult conversation with your manager. Honesty is always the best policy and supports your professional integrity.

10) Treat your manager as you would be treated. Be thankful for the Golden Rule and live it as a foundation for daily interactions.

ACKNOWLEDGMENTS

Below is a list of manager-leaders to whom I reported at various times throughout my career. All these people had an influence on my sales management development. Some had more positive impact than others, yet all contributed to my understanding of sales management as a truly unique and gratifying career option.

I am grateful to all listed for helping me learn what to do, as I am equally thankful to them for helping me learn what not to do. I appreciate the time they spent with me along the way.

Richard "Dick" Stern

Gerry Rovensky

Keith Davis

Bob Siuda

Ed Shivitz

Greg Linnerooth

Mark Hawley

Scott Schaffer

Mike Hiskett

Jim Behling

Virginia Mechnig

Bob Trombetta

Bill Rauscher

Bill Holtry

Christine Hierl

Joe Dillelo

Ranada Anderson

John Holbrook

Thomas Brooks

Dave Pauldine

Steve Riehs

Christopher Caywood

Adrian Marrullier

Mike Bisk

Ken Maher

Dr. Fletcher Lamkin

CPSIA information can be obtained
at www.ICGtesting.com
Printed in the USA
LVHW010814080720
660058LV00002B/77